GA$
SMART$

CUT YOUR
GAS BILLS
BY A
THIRD!

GA$ SMART$

CUT YOUR GAS BILLS BY A THIRD!

HUNDREDS OF SMALL WAYS TO SAVE BIG AT THE PUMP

RONALD M. WEIERS, PhD

Aadamsmedia
Avon, Massachusetts

Published by
Adams Media, a division of F+W Media, Inc.
57 Littlefield Street, Avon, MA 02322. U.S.A.
www.adamsmedia.com

Contains material adapted and abridged from *365 Ways to Save Gas: Everyday Tips to Stretch
Your Dollar*, by Ronald M. Weiers, PhD, copyright © 2006 by Ronald M. Weiers, ISBN 10:
0756627346, ISBN 13: 9780756627348.

ISBN 10: 1-4405-0049-5
ISBN 13: 978-1-4405-0049-7
eISBN 10: 1-4405-1081-4
eISBN 13: 978-1-4405-1081-6

Printed in the United States of America.

10   9   8   7   6   5   4   3   2   1

**Library of Congress Cataloging-in-
Publication Data**
Weiers, Ronald M.
Ga$ smart$ / Ronald M. Weiers.
p. cm.
"Contains material adapted and abridged from
*365 Ways to Save Gas: Everyday Tips to Stretch
Your Dollar*, by Ronald M. Weiers."
Includes index.
ISBN-13: 978-1-4405-0049-7
ISBN-13: 978-1-4405-1081-6 (ebk.)
ISBN-10: 1-4405-0049-5
ISBN-10: 1-4405-1081-4 (ebk.)
1. Automobiles—Fuel consumption.
2. Automobile driving—Economic aspects. I.
Title. II. Title: Gas smarts.
TL151.6.W453 2011
629.25'3—dc22
2011006249

To the memory of our wonderful son, Bob.

Contents

Introduction:
Getting Serious about Saving

In October 1991, a gigantic storm hit the entire East Coast. The storm had many elements that, had they occurred alone, would have been inconsequential. However, the synergy of their combined effects generated death, devastation, and destruction up and down the Eastern Atlantic Seaboard. The U.S. National Weather Service labeled it "the perfect storm," and it inspired both a novel and a movie by the same name. What does this have to do with your saving money at the gas pump? Read on.

"Perfect" Oil Storms—Past and Future

As with our annual Atlantic hurricane and East-Coast nor'easter seasons, we continually face the possibility of new energy storms—perfect oil storms—that involve oil consumption, availability, and price. When they arrive, such oil storms can be prolonged and painful, and may involve many elements, including geopolitical events and global conflicts, reliance on imported oil, national security and terrorism issues, concerns about the environment and global warming, hurricanes and other weather catastrophes, the threat of supply disruptions, the precarious state of our national economy, our own job uncertainties and household budgets, and our historical national tendency to aspire to vehicles that are bigger and faster.

The personal impact of these "perfect" oil storms is most apparent when we visit the gas pump and spend $60 or more to fill our tank. Between 2002 and the middle of 2006, the average retail price for a gallon of unleaded gasoline went from under $1.50 to nearly $3.00, in 2008 many Americans were paying well over $4.00 per gallon, and the overall upward trend will not be going away anytime soon. There will be price valleys that invite complacency as well as price spikes that lead to panic at the pump, but during these ups and downs the price of gas will continue its persistently upward long-term trend. Future and seemingly unrelated national and global events will occasionally combine to generate future price spikes that will make those $4 per gallon days seem like a bargain, and our economic and national security pains could be much worse than we're already experiencing. At this writing, the average retail prices of different grades of gasoline are regularly published in *USA Today*, placing the price of gasoline somewhere near the weather forecast in terms of its importance to our daily lives and activities.

What Can You Do Today?

Your credit cards are drained, your checkbook is thin, your savings are depleted, and the financial news is depressing, yet those gasoline prices keep cycling ever upward. What can you do? You can and should use your political voice to support candidates and policies that encourage more efficient use of that precious oil, but keep in mind that we're dealing with a finite natural resource that will eventually disappear.

You can also lend support to politicians and organizations dedicated to finding fuel and propulsion alternatives. This is a worthy goal, but it takes time. As much as we'd like, neither the four-wheeled perpetual motion machine nor the nuclear-powered vehicle is anywhere in sight. However, progress is being made, and future generations will read their history books and see today's vehicles in the same light as we now view primitive machines from the early 1900s.

In the meantime, and for the purposes of this book, let's focus on the part of the problem where each of us can have a direct, immediate, and meaningful impact: getting better fuel efficiency and using other tricks to save our hard-earned money at the gas pump. To start saving money today, consider that what you spend on fuel is largely a function of two very simple factors: *what* you drive and *how* you drive. In this book, we will discuss both, but for reasons discussed in the next section, we will especially emphasize the latter.

The Basics of the Book

Barring some unforeseen event, like a big lottery win or an off-season visit from Santa, the vehicle parked in your driveway right now is the same vehicle that will be parked there when you wake up tomorrow morning. For most of us, the money's just not there for us to hop out of bed tomorrow and buy a new car, be it a new hybrid or a used Hummer. Ideally, you'll purchase a more fuel-efficient vehicle when replacement time comes. Until then, we want to help you do the best you can with what you have, and that's an important reason for these chapters and the order in which they are presented:

Chapters 1 through 3 focus on your driving and use of any vehicle, especially the one you're already driving. Chapters 4 and 5 will guide you when you are able to enter the marketplace and replace your current vehicle, and Chapter 6 discusses some of the aftermarket accessories that could affect the fuel efficiency of either your current vehicle or the one that's waiting for you in a future showroom. Appendices A and B briefly address specific considerations and specialized strategies for two kinds of vehicles that are of particular importance: the sports-utility vehicle (SUV) and the hybrid. Appendix C discusses how the practices advised in this book can help you by increasing both the life of your car and the value it returns when you eventually sell it or trade it in. Appendix D addresses the somewhat controversial practice known as "hypermiling," while Appendices E and F discuss a variety of more "macro" matters, including the environment, reducing petroleum demand, fuel prices in the United States compared to Europe, some specific global threats involving our oil supplies, and the promise of new technologies not yet in the showroom.

Why Should You Read This Book?

Sure, you've seen news features, brochures, and televised talking heads galore, and they all spout general ideas for saving money at the gas pump. Your first thought might be, "Hey, I've already had people tell me how to get more miles out of my gas dollar, so why should I spend money on a book instead of a couple gallons of gas?" There are three reasons why this book is important to you:

Practical Tips, Not Just General Advice. There's a lot more to saving gas than just pumping up your tires and obeying the speed limits. While others give you general tips, like "conserve momentum," *Ga$ Smart$* takes you to a completely different level—a level that gives you many specific and sometimes unintuitive tips on actually implementing such general advice as conserving momentum. Just a few examples are the 3-second following-distance rule, looking beyond the vehicle immediately ahead, and taking advantage of the pavement weight sensors at traffic signals. Where others would essentially tell their football team to "complete a long pass and score," *Ga$ Smart$* is like the meticulous coach who provides exact details as to how the receiver will get open, how the passer will trick the defense into thinking a different play is being run, and how the offensive line will protect the passer long enough for the receiver to sprint all the way to the end zone to complete the score. Where the brochures and the talking heads just give you the job description, we give you the tools to get the job done.

Even Small Improvements Add Up to a Big Difference. The Japanese call it "Kaizen"—achieving greater quality and efficiency through continual process improvement, even if by small increments. Like anything else you do or build, driving your car is a process that you can continually improve. Every time you accelerate, brake, shift gears, approach an intersection, or make your daily commute, try to do so just a little more efficiently than you did the time before. It's a different mindset and there's some philosophy involved, but you may find it beneficial in your everyday life as well as in your driving. Some of the tips are extremely important, others may be viewed as marginal—but they all take you in the same worthy direction: saving your gas money, helping your country toward greater energy independence, and reducing the wear and tear we are placing upon our planet.

Don't Just Save Gas—Save Lives Too! Aggressive driving is one of the leading causes of automotive injuries and fatalities. In addition to being rude, thoughtless, and dangerous, aggressive driving is also highly inefficient. As he speeds, weaves, and otherwise endangers innocent lives, the aggressive driver is also wasting fuel and making his country even more dependent on the nations from which we import most of the expensive oil from which his gasoline is made. Be safe, be efficient, and avoid both aggressive driving and aggressive drivers. Follow the advice in *Ga$ Smart$*: Just leave home ten minutes earlier and take it easy along the way.

Regardless of where you are and what you're driving, you'll find within these pages many ideas to help you travel longer distances between those ever-more-expensive fill-ups. There will be some tips that might, at first glance, seem relatively insignificant. There will be others that will stand out as being a "big stick" in their effect on helping you save gasoline and money. However, when you combine and apply them all, you will have the equivalent of your own "perfect storm" of personal response to rising fuel prices and their effect on your budget. Best wishes for happy, safe, and efficient motoring.

CHAPTER 1

Driving Efficiently

You've got to care.

The most important thing to remember about driving efficiently is that you have to *care* about driving efficiently. Improving your fuel economy means paying attention to all the little things that add up to big savings, and this requires a little effort on your part. If you care about saving gas, money, and the environment, then make a commitment to doing the little things—starting today.

In heavy traffic, get braking clues from the cars ahead.

In heavy stop-and-go traffic, don't just watch the vehicle immediately in front of you. Whenever possible, use the brake lights of those even farther ahead as a "countdown" sequence to help you anticipate upcoming starts and stops. In a tunnel, look for reflections on walls and ceilings. On rainy days, brake lights at least two vehicles ahead can be seen by looking beneath the vehicle directly ahead. The high-mounted center brake lights on today's vehicles makes this strategy even easier to use. By starting a little sooner, going a little slower, and stopping a little later, you can better maintain momentum and smoothness. You also minimize use of one of your biggest efficiency foes, the dreaded brake pedal.

Be already moving when you start to move.

Yes, this sounds like something Yogi Berra would say, but it is a valid piece of advice, nonetheless. You can reduce both fuel consumption and wear on your car if you're moving even slowly when you begin to accelerate. This applies to many different kinds of traffic situations. For example, if you have automatic transmission and the road is level or downhill, allow your engine's idle speed to get you moving slowly before you actually step on the accelerator. When it comes to fuel efficiency, momentum is precious and we try to preserve it whenever we can.

Relax in the vehicular parade.

It's inevitable. At some point, you will be trapped within a stream of vehicles on a curvy road or in a no-passing zone. Regardless of what you say or do, you will have absolutely no control over your rate of progress during this time. In this situation, the typical driver alternates between the accelerator pedal and brake pedal as though they were buttons on a keyboard. This jerky driving is very inefficient. Your best strategy is to relax, listen to some music, and remember that you will eventually be the person at the beginning of the parade.

When you're the leader of the parade.

Sometimes while driving along at a perfectly moderate and efficient speed, you'll find yourself at the head of the vehicular stream in which there is no opportunity for anyone to pass. If you're being pressured from behind, you can try speeding up a little, but chances are the other driver will do the same and stay on your back bumper anyway. Don't give in to the pressure by driving at unsafe or illegal speeds. As the leader of a pack that is exceeding the speed limit, you are the one most likely to get the speeding ticket. If you're uncomfortable, this could be a good time to pull over for a moment and allow someone else to lead the parade, as the cost of a speeding ticket or boosted insurance rate could buy a fair amount of fuel.

Be courteous and patient.

This may sound like part of a scouting pledge, but it makes an incredible difference in the way you drive and the efficiency you achieve while doing so. Unless you're an ambulance driver, an extra five or ten minutes isn't going to make much of a difference. You'll get there when you get there.

Don't drive when you're angry.

Angry people are neither smooth nor fun to be around, especially when they're driving. Angry driving means a lot of speed, acceleration, and braking, all of which waste fuel. According to the EPA, aggressive driving can reduce gas mileage by 33 percent at highway speeds and 5 percent around town. As an angry driver, you may also experience negative consequences if you happen to encounter someone in a similar mood who wishes to race or to rage. Count to ten, meditate, or forget about being angry until you get where you're going.

Slowing for the dreaded tunnel.

Anticipate the fact that vehicles ahead will almost certainly slow down as they approach a tunnel, this despite the ever-present signs that say "Maintain Speed Through Tunnel." It's human nature, and it often applies to bridges as well. Although I hate to provide advice that could reinforce an already unfortunate road phenomenon, you should consider slowing down early so you won't have to brake to avoid those who will be slowing down in front of you.

Why slower is better.

Your car's air resistance goes up a lot quicker than your speed, and going faster at highway speeds is like stacking fishing boats on top of your car. A mere 10 percent increase in speed (e.g., from 50 to 55 mph) requires a whopping 33 percent increase in the horsepower needed to overcome air resistance! In tests using a 2001 Chevrolet Malibu (estimated EPA highway mpg: 29), the car got 35 mpg at a steady 55 mph, compared to just 25 mpg at a steady 70 mph. As always, be safe: when it's neither practical nor safe to maintain super-efficient speeds, just do the next best thing and travel as moderately as possible without becoming a safety hazard or inviting road rage. (A note for the math-inclined: The necessary horsepower to overcome air resistance is a cube function of speed, so if you increase your speed by 20 percent, the horsepower multiple will then be 1.20^3, or 1.73—you'll need 73 percent more horsepower than was required at the more efficient speed.)

Obey the speed limits.

Speed limits exist for safety reasons, but they contribute to fuel economy as well. Many drivers routinely exceed speed limits, assuming that either they won't get caught or that police officers will cut them a little slack. In doing so, they're wasting fuel and risking accidents or speeding tickets that could boost their insurance premiums by an increment far beyond what it costs for either fuel or traffic court. If the speed limit is 60 mph, exceeding it can cost a lot of gas—according to the EPA, each 5 mph you drive over 60 mph can reduce your fuel economy by about 8 percent, and that equates to a pretty hefty discount at the pump.

The invisible cop behind you.

Have you noticed how your driving behavior changes drastically when a police patrol car is in the vicinity? Police officers report noticeable differences in how they are treated when they're off-duty and driving their personal vehicle as opposed to their patrol cars.

None of us can truly imagine how frustrated they must become when somebody cuts them off while they're driving their family wagon to the mall. The point of this discussion is this: for best efficiency, drive as though a patrol car is behind you. If that doesn't impress you, pretend your mother-in-law is in the back seat.

Be gentle and smooth.

This title might imply some degree of inappropriateness for a family-rated book. However, the very best thing you can do to get the most miles per gallon from your vehicle is to be gentle and smooth in everything you do. You should pretend you have two raw eggs in the car—one resting on the accelerator pedal and the other resting on the brake pedal. Only rarely, when you really do need to get from point A to point B in minimum time, should you pretend that these eggs are hard-boiled.

The cup of coffee on the dash.

Another way to apply the "gentle-and-smooth" rule is to pretend you have a full-to-the-brim cup of hot coffee on the dashboard. (If you're a multitasking commuter in an older car without today's standard twenty-seven cup holders, this might actually be true.) Regardless, you should drive as though the full cup is sitting there and you are trying to avoid spilling any of its contents.

Accelerate moderately.

Most activities we enjoy are good for us, in moderation. The same is true for acceleration—too slow and we spend extra time and distance in the lower, less efficient gears; too fast and we use excessive energy with both the engine and transmission operating in inefficient modes. If you drive a manual, shift up as soon as the engine will accept the greater load of the higher gear. If you drive an automatic, keep a light foot on the gas and accelerate somewhere between moderately and briskly.

Avoid panic stops.

Panic stops are always necessary at the time—you make them to avoid accidents. However, think about what you might have done to avoid being in that situation where the panic stop became necessary. A good clue to such abruptness in your driving is the occasional passenger with whom you may be traveling. If you often see this person extending his or her foot as if to press an imaginary brake pedal, you're probably driving neither patiently nor smoothly. If you find it extremely difficult to find a passenger to ride with you at all, you may wish to read this chapter of the book a few more times.

Don't be a brake-tapper.

This is the world's most expensive magic trick. You tap the brake pedal and—presto—gasoline is transformed into brake-pad heat and dust. Every time you step on the brake, you're killing momentum the engine worked hard to generate in the first place. Some people seem to touch their brake pedal at virtually every turn in the road, like a cowhand tipping his hat to passersby on the street. Minimize brake applications by anticipating what's ahead, taking your foot off the accelerator early, and allowing the car to slow down on its own.

When you're following a brake-tapper.

First of all, you should have left home 10 seconds earlier. However, since you didn't, the next best thing is to back off a little and give the car ahead extra space. Otherwise you'll end up having to duplicate their jerky and inefficient behavior.

That's not a footrest!

Don't laugh. A lot of people rest their foot on the clutch or brake pedal without realizing it, and this can reduce fuel efficiency through clutch slippage or inadvertent braking. In the latter case, you end up slowing the car down with one foot while you're asking it to move with the other. You wouldn't turn on your home heating and air conditioning at the same time, so why ask your car to do the automotive equivalent?

Don't tailgate.

This works well in NASCAR and Formula One, but tailgating on the highway can involve a lot of inefficient braking and accelerating. Furthermore, it is dangerous. We've all read about twenty-vehicle pile-ups that were "caused" by the sudden appearance of a patch of fog. Instead of blaming the fog, we should point the finger at people who are driving closer together than their reaction times and braking distances can support. On a related note: don't attempt to save fuel by "drafting" behind big-rig trucks. Your sedan can become a convertible very quickly if you end up getting pushed into the back of one.

When you're being tailgated.

No matter how fast we go, there's always someone who wants to go faster, and they always seem to end up on our back bumper. If the only thing you can see in your rear-view mirror is the word "Kenworth" spelled backwards, either speed up or move over, whichever can happen safer and sooner. Some truckers either don't know or don't care about the gargantuan distance it takes to slow down when the vehicle in front must stop or slow down because of an emergency or other event ahead. If you have nowhere to escape, don't hesitate to put on the four-way flashers to call attention to the situation and perhaps dissuade the person from his reckless behavior. Regardless of what kind of vehicle is on your rear bumper, it's both prudent and fuel efficient to simply get out of the way and allow him to proceed more quickly to the destination that is obviously so important to him.

Don't get "boxed-in."

In track events, runners often get "boxed in" by slower traffic. The same thing happens on the highway and, by anticipating who is going to be where and when, you can move into the passing lane and overtake the slower traffic without having to interrupt your all-important momentum. The key is being aware of the present situation and being able to visualize the immediate future. Of course, being boxed in behind a Winnebago pulling a U-Haul trailer will lead to low speeds and therefore high fuel efficiency, but most of us need to get where we're going sometime this week.

The 3-second rule.

To allow time for slowing down early, accelerating early, and continuing your momentum as much as possible, try to stay at least 3 seconds behind the vehicle ahead. This should provide sufficient time and space in which to react to events taking place in front of you. In general, when the vehicle in front passes an expansion strip or other marking on the road, you should get there no sooner than 3 seconds later. This is good for safety as well as fuel efficiency. If the person behind you is closer than 3 seconds behind, you may need to expand your own front zone to compensate for the inadequacy of his. Be sure to increase your following distance in slippery conditions, poor visibility, or bad weather.

Where will you be in 15 seconds?

By considering where you and your fellow travelers will be in another 15 seconds, you're doing the equivalent of thinking more moves ahead in a chess game. With such advance notice, you can better avoid getting "boxed-in" behind slower vehicles, and you can more effectively prepare for hills, traffic signals, and nearly anything else that calls for changing either your speed or your lane in order to conserve momentum and reduce fuel consumption.

Get clues from the signs.

Observe roadside signs for clues as to what's coming up, and respond accordingly. If a sign says "School Zone Ahead," for example, lift from the accelerator immediately and slow down with little or no braking. The speed limit ahead will undoubtedly be extremely low. When you see a sign with a large zig-zagging arrow on it, realize that a curvy road lies ahead, and you should gradually and smoothly navigate the curves rather than charge each one only to hit the brakes on the way through. Whether the sign says "Stop Sign Ahead" or "Steep Hill, Trucks Gear Down," you can be sure of one thing: the majority of signs you see will be providing early warning to lighten your right foot. There aren't many signs that will be telling you to accelerate.

Use your mirrors.

If you're driving efficiently, a lot of the action may be taking place behind you or next to you. Be sure the center and side-view mirrors are properly adjusted, and make frequent use of them to monitor activities to the rear and on both sides. In traffic, before you touch the brake, quickly glance at the rear-view mirror to make sure a quick stop won't cause an accident because the person behind is following too closely. Even in light traffic, you must often base safe and fuel-efficient decisions on what the people around you are doing.

Brake gradually.

For both efficiency and increased life of your brakes and their components, brake gradually if you have to brake at all. Hitting the brakes kills your momentum, so apply them sparingly. But by all means, for safety's sake, apply them when you have to.

Braking: was this really necessary?

Get into the habit of asking yourself how you might have avoided or minimized your use of the brake. Planning a little further ahead and better anticipating traffic conditions can save your brakes, your momentum, and your gas.

Pretend you have no brakes at all.

One approach to the mindset of minimizing brake use is to pretend you have no brakes at all, and drive accordingly. However, don't shift down to use engine braking instead. Also, it's important that you be prepared to immediately escape from the "pretend" concept and actually use the brakes when you really need them. You may find it interesting that two motorists once drove from Detroit to Los Angeles without using their brakes at all. The brakes had been sealed by a Detroit testing laboratory and could have been used in an emergency, but they were never applied even once during the entire trip.

Lifting from the accelerator.

When lifting your foot from the accelerator, ask yourself if you might have been able to do this a little sooner by better anticipating the environment ahead and the actions of the vehicles you've been following.

Beware of potholes and road debris.

Wheel alignment and front-end components can suffer expensive and gas-wasting damage when you hit a tooth-jarring pothole or run over an abandoned exhaust muffler. By staying at least 3 seconds behind the vehicle in front, you're in a better position to see and avoid such obstacles.

Where are your tires?

Depending on where you parked last night, they're probably still on your car. However, this is not good enough. You should have a sense of the exact locations where your tires will be contacting the road. On a rainy day, you can practice by doing such things as looking in the mirror to see where your tracks are relative to those of a vehicle that has gone before, or aiming at the edge of a marking or imperfection in the road to see how close you can come to passing directly over a selected portion of it. Besides making you more adept at maneuvering around potholes, road debris, and wayward forest creatures, you'll be better able to minimize rolling resistance by using the lane and road advice that follows.

Avoid lane grooves in the rain.

Rough, harsh road surfaces increase rolling resistance and reduce fuel efficiency. Due to factors like truck traffic, road maintenance, and the use of studded snow tires in some locales, some parts of the lane may be smoother than others, and can give you an efficiency advantage. Also, because of heavy use, some lanes may even have a parallel set of grooves worn into them. Try to avoid these grooves when it's raining, since they gather additional water that will have to be pushed out of the way by your tires. This increases rolling resistance, fuel consumption, and the potential for hydroplaning.

Drive on the flatter surface.

Most roads have a slight amount of tilt or "camber" at the edge to assist with water drainage during rain conditions. If you drive in this portion of your lane, your car will tend to "tilt" a tiny bit, requiring some corrective steering to overcome this effect. As a result, your tires will be working a little harder in order to prevent you from drifting in the direction of the tilt, and this will lead to more tire wear, greater rolling resistance, and higher fuel consumption.

On curves, favor the inside line.

The shortest distance between two points is a straight line. Unless you're in Iowa, you're probably not going to see many roads that offer this advantage. Nevertheless, you can shorten the distance of your journey just a little by slightly favoring the inside part of the lane when rounding curves. But be safe about it, because adjacent vehicles and oncoming traffic won't care about your fuel-efficient driving.

Minimize use of auxiliary lighting.

If you have auxiliary lights on the front of your vehicle, don't bother using them unless they're really necessary for good vision in dark, foggy weather. Your engine must consume gasoline to produce the electricity they require.

Leaving the construction zone.

In many locales, you are required to turn on headlights while traveling through highway construction zones. When leaving the zone, don't forget to save some energy by turning them off again.

After the tunnel.

It's a safe idea to use headlamps in a tunnel whether required or not. Save energy by turning the lights off as you leave the tunnel—don't wait for the "are your lights still on?" reminder that's often a quarter-mile past the tunnel exit.

In downhill gridlock, shut off and drift.

We've all encountered the accident or emergency situation where cars are completely stopped, doors are open, and people are walking around asking each other what's going on up ahead. You may not want to walk around and make new friends, but at least save gas by shutting off the engine. If the orientation happens to be downhill and you have a manual transmission, save even more gas by just drifting the few feet at a time that occasional traffic movement might require. This is not recommended for automatics, the moving parts of which often require the circulation of transmission fluid or engine coolant to dissipate the heat generated by their internal components. Stay safe—be sure your brake lights come on even when the ignition is off, and keep in mind that, without engine assistance, the power steering and power brakes will require more force to operate.

Minimize rear-window defrosting.

If you have a rear-window defrosting system with its maze of wires across the window, don't use it any more than you have to. It uses a lot of electricity, so turn it off as soon as the window is clear. If there's snow and ice on the rear window, give the defroster a hand by spending a half-minute or so removing these layers with a brush or scraper.

Lay off the electric seat warmer.

This is another horrendous electricity consumer and, if your car has this feature, either minimize its use or don't use it at all.

Minimize the horn.

Regardless of what act of stupidity some other driver performs, try to resist honking the horn (or using other forms of communication) to send him a message. There are times when the horn is necessary for safety purposes, but these are few and far between. Honking the horn is not only going to irritate those around you, it will probably make your own mood even worse, and the end result will be fuel inefficiency accompanied by a possible migraine. If that argument doesn't suffice, keep in mind that the horn uses electricity—and electricity uses gas.

Lower the antenna if it's not in use.

Unless you have an exterior radio antenna that automatically sprouts from the fender when the sound system is turned on, lower the antenna if you're just going to listen to a CD. There will be slightly less air resistance and, if you drive far enough, you'll save enough fuel to pay for the CD.

Low speeds: spare the air and open the windows.

If you're traveling at relatively low speeds, such as under 45 or 50 miles per hour, consider lowering the windows instead of using the air conditioning. At these speeds, there is relatively little air resistance so the loss of aerodynamics will not be very costly to your fuel efficiency.

Higher speeds: spare the windows and use the air.

Even the most aerodynamic of cars become much less so when you open the windows at higher speeds (above 45 or 50 miles per hour). Under these conditions, energy saved by having low air drag will completely or greatly offset the energy consumed by the air conditioning system.

For die-hards only: spare the windows *and* the air.

The most efficient mode of all, regardless of speed, is to keep the windows raised and the air conditioning turned off. This is only for the most hardy individuals, or for those trying to make it home on fumes. For everyday driving, prudent use of windows or air conditioning is a lot cheaper than having to pay for that trip to the emergency room for treatment of heat exhaustion. If you don't want to completely close the windows, opening the rear ones slightly will not increase air drag as much as opening the front ones.

Use and enjoy the sunroof.

A sunroof with a proper wind deflector can greatly improve ventilation at most speeds below interstate level, and with relatively little additional aerodynamic drag. The combination of the open sunroof and rear windows that are only very slightly opened can enhance the flow of air into and through the car. When it's not terribly hot outside, this is a fuel-saving alternative to any of the windows-versus-air strategies.

Ventilate before turning on the air.

If you're going to use the air conditioning, give it a head start by briefly opening the windows and running the ventilation fan. This will clear out much of the built-up heat within the car and the ventilation system, so your car will cool off more quickly, and you'll save some gas.

Use the "recirculate" mode.

Regardless of what it's called or what symbol might be on the control button, your air conditioning system will likely have a mode in which most of the air is being recirculated instead of being brought in from the outside. As a result, the air conditioning will not have to work as hard, and you will not have to buy as much fuel.

Turning and temperature changes.

Don't be fooled into cranking up the air conditioner immediately after turning a corner. The temperature has not really increased. The car is now pointed in a different direction, but the air within it is still aimed in the same direction it was before the turn. It's similar to what happens when we quickly rotate a glass of orange juice—although we rotate the glass, the orange juice within tends not to rotate along with it. Anyway, the temperatures will quickly balance out and you and your passenger will soon enjoy your previous levels of comfort—at least until the next corner.

Avoid extended idling.

If you're going to be stopped for a minute or more, save gas by shutting off the engine. At first, this may seem an unnatural thing to be doing, but it does save gas. According to Natural Resources Canada, idling a 3-liter engine for 10 minutes uses about 1/3 quart of gasoline.

Convertibles: battling the buffeting.

Convertibles encounter less air resistance and are more fuel efficient when their tops are up. At low speeds, the penalty is less severe, but at highway speeds, air turbulence greatly increases aerodynamic drag and reduces fuel economy. Some models have a shield behind the driver and passenger that can help offset this problem during top-down highway travel. If your convertible does not have one, you can reduce turbulence by fully or partially raising one or both of the side windows. You may have to experiment to achieve the best results, depending on speed of travel and the presence of crosswinds. Anyway, don't feel too guilty when your top is down—at least you're having fun and you're not using the air conditioning.

Avoid the pancake idle.

The remote starter and breakfast-table warm-up might make your car comfortably toasty by the time you've finished your pancakes, but you've been getting zero miles per gallon in the process. It's much more efficient to start out from cold and gradually warm up the whole car (i.e., more than just the engine and transmission) as you travel.

The doggy in the window.

For purposes not fully understood, every dog who has ever been in a car enjoys riding along with his head sticking out of the window, sometimes very far out of the window. Whether you have a Chihuahua or a Saint Bernard, the combination of the open window and the dog's head will increase air resistance and reduce fuel efficiency. For better fuel efficiency and for your pet's safety, consider lowering the window just far enough that he can see well and is able to sniff whatever it is he sniffs out there.

Footwear makes a difference.

Fashionable shoes or boots with high heels can make it more difficult for you to perform the smooth and precise applications of brake, clutch, and accelerator that efficient driving demands. Unfashionable footwear such as steel-toe work boots might be heavy as well as awkward, and you could end up exerting more force than you realize on the accelerator pedal—and we know that a heavy foot on the accelerator is not a good thing for fuel efficiency. You don't need to emulate Formula One competitors in choosing specialized footwear for driving, but opt for comfortable shoes that aren't awkward or heavy. You can always change into the footwear required by your destination when you arrive at your destination.

Dress for efficiency.

Naturally, there will be occasions when the business suit is a necessity instead of an option, and you'll have no choice but to use the air conditioning to keep cool. However, in general, consider the temperatures you'll encounter during your trip, then dress accordingly so you can reduce energy consumption by the air conditioning and heating systems.

Use either a hands-free cell phone or no phone.

In some jurisdictions, drivers of vehicles in motion must use only cell phones designed for hands-free operation. In any case, the hands-free cell phone reduces the potential for distractions that could interfere with safe and efficient driving, and it's a must-have item if you're driving a manual transmission. Note that some jurisdictions may ban any type of cell phone use while you are driving, so be sure to save gas by shutting off the engine when you pull over to talk. Researchers at the National Highway Traffic Safety Institute estimate that drivers talking on their cell phone are four times as likely to crash as other drivers, and they are as likely to cause an accident as someone with a blood alcohol content (BAC) of 0.08 percent, the level at which you can be arrested for driving under the influence in most of the United States.

Texting costs fuel and lives.

Multitasking can be good if you're at work or on the computer, but it is both fuel-inefficient and deadly on the highway. As a distraction, texting is even more dangerous than talking on a cell phone. As you drive down the interstate looking for a tiny button on that miniature keyboard, your car is traveling the length of football field every three seconds, and trees, bridge abutments, and big-rig drivers will not have much control over where they are when you suddenly arrive in front of them. Speaking of the big rigs, a study by the Virginia Tech Transportation Institute found that truckers are 23 times more likely to cause an accident while sending text messages. To save both your life and your gasoline, don't text while driving, and keep your eyes wide open for those around you who are.

Where are those buttons and switches?

Further reduce potential distractions by familiarizing yourself with all of the control buttons and switches located on your vehicle's steering wheel, steering column, and instrument panel. Controls for the entertainment system tend to be especially confusing for many of us, and it's difficult to drive either safely or efficiently when you're searching for the volume control or trying to figure out how to skip to the next CD or MP3 track. It is absolutely essential that you be able to immediately locate and activate the emergency flasher switch whenever the situation demands, such as coming upon an accident scene or obstruction. Advance notice to motorists behind you will help the rear of your car retain the aerodynamic shape it had when it left the factory.

Rush hour: use the HOV lane.

During rush hour, if there is a high-occupancy-vehicle (HOV) lane and you are eligible to use it, be sure to do so. Eligibility may require a minimum number of occupants, of course, but some locales also allow access to solo drivers of certain hybrid vehicles. Obey the law and don't consider loading your car with mannequins or cardboard celebrities—it's clever, but authorities already know about this trick.

Stopping on the right.

Try to frequent filling stations, rest areas, and restaurants that are on the right. This makes it easier and more efficient when you return to the highway.

Lost? Ask, don't wander.

For some, this is against our nature, reputedly especially so for males, but stopping and asking for directions uses less fuel than wandering around and trying to find your own way. When stopping for your inquiry, try to favor people and places located adjacent to the lane in which you are traveling. As with the previous tip, this makes it easier and more efficient to return to the highway and resume your journey.

Skip a gear.

Although some high school students have likely flunked Driver's Ed for skipping a gear in the teacher's manual-transmission car, this strategy can be useful. For example, when accelerating downhill we can reduce the wasteful throttle manipulations involved in the ritual of shifting through all the gears when the full sequence is not really necessary. Going from first to third or from third to fifth can save fuel—but be careful to keep a light foot on the accelerator so you don't lug the engine (drive in too high a gear with a power demand that's too great for your speed).

Get into top gear quickly.

Whether driving a manual or an automatic, get into top gear as soon as possible, especially when the road is level or you are headed downhill. With a manual, use a light foot on the accelerator and shift up to the next gear as soon as the engine will accept the increased load. With an automatic, the advice is similar, but you need only concentrate on the lightness of your foot on the accelerator—apply pressure that is firm but steady. If you're headed up a steep hill, be patient and keep in mind that your goal of reaching top gear may be either impossible or inefficient under these conditions.

Use the cruise control wisely.

As befits its purpose, cruise control maintains a steady speed. This is good when you're on a fairly level road with few curves and the traffic is relatively light. The device also helps you avoid those forgetful periods when you inadvertently exceed the speed limit and risk the expense of a ticket. However, its good intentions can sometimes prove inefficient, such as when it applies the pre-set speed in whisking you over the peak of a hill only to force you to waste energy by braking excessively on the way down the other side. When you're climbing a hill, the cruise control will sometimes downshift to a less efficient gear when you could have simply slowed down by one or two mph and stayed in top gear.

Disengaging the cruise control.

Cruise controls disengage when you press the brake, the clutch (manual transmission), or the "off" switch. If you must disengage by using the brake, don't tap or press the pedal any harder than necessary for safety. Remember, brakes use gas by taking away the valuable momentum your engine labored to generate. If you've looked ahead and anticipated disengagement of the cruise control, you can save both gas and brake wear by simply using the "off" switch.

Pseudo cruise control.

If you don't have cruise control, do the next best thing—tag along a safe and generous distance behind someone who does, and who is traveling at a safe and efficient speed.

Speedometer check: how fast are you really going?

Speedometer accuracy can vary slightly from one vehicle to the next. Furthermore, the diameter of your tires will decrease slightly as the result of normal wear. As a result you may be traveling faster or slower than your speedometer indicates. If there are mileposts along the highway, and you have a watch with a chronograph feature, measure how many seconds it takes for you to get from one milepost to the next. At 60 miles per hour, it should take 60 seconds (i.e., 3600 seconds in an hour, divided by 60 mph) to cover the mile.

When does the automatic lock up?

Many modern automatic transmissions have a lock-up feature that eliminates torque converter slippage under light load once you've reached a certain speed in top gear. When engaged, this provides a direct connection between the engine and the transmission output shaft(s) and makes you just as efficient as someone driving a manual. If, under light load, the lock-up engages at 46 miles per hour, traveling at 45 mph doesn't make much sense. If, in response to slight downward or upward accelerator movement, the tachometer and speedometer needles move slightly upward or downward together, you're locked up. If not, you're not.

Use the top gear override switch.

When climbing a grade, you'll sometimes experience a situation known as "hunting," whereby the automatic transmission keeps changing its mind as to which gear it wants to have engaged. When this happens, press the override switch that tells it to remain in the lower gear instead of jumping back forth between it and the next one up. This switch is typically located on the transmission shift lever. You'll not only save fuel, but you'll help your transmission last longer. Just remember to disengage the override switch when hunting season is over.

Don't downshift to slow down.

Not only does this waste gas, but brake pads are much cheaper than engine and transmission parts. So use the brakes for the function for which they were designed, but remember to use them as little as possible.

Give the weight sensor time to think.

You're leaving the shopping mall, traveling uphill, and yours is the first car approaching the red light where you'll be turning left. Chances are there is a sensor in the pavement to tell the signal system you are present and that you'll be needing a green light. If you move slowly after touching the sensor, you'll have an opportunity to keep moving instead of doing an unnecessary stop and start. This works at other kinds of intersections as well, but beware of motorists who think they "own" their light for a few seconds after it turns red.

Glide over the speed bumps.

Speed bumps are an effective way to discourage dangerous speeding in parking lots and other areas. However, instead of charging up to a speed bump, hitting the brakes, then slowly traversing the bump, there's a more fuel efficient way of handling the situation. If you're in a mall parking lot, you should be traveling slowly anyway, so it's not much more effort to simply remove your foot from the accelerator very early and slow down before you arrive at the speed bump. The experience will still not be a pleasant one, but at least you will have avoided using the brakes and wasting fuel and momentum.

Drive straight.

Concentrate on the direction you're headed and avoid drifting back and forth within your lane. These sideward drifts can be caused by various sources of inattention, including the feeling that it's necessary to make frequent eye contact when conversing with a passenger. Unnecessary and frequent sideward movements reduce fuel efficiency in two ways—they increase the distance you end up traveling, and your tires will have greater rolling resistance because they have to resist more sideward forces in addition to the normal directional force required just to travel in a straight line.

Ease into the downhill starts.

At a downhill stop sign or signal, drift just a little before you engage the clutch or press the accelerator. Use gravity to help you save gas as well as wear and tear on your clutch and transmission components.

Hold your own on uphill starts.

If you drive a manual transmission with a pull-up handbrake, use the handbrake to hold your position, then simultaneously release the handbrake, engage the clutch, and press on the accelerator when traffic clears or the signal changes. As beginning drivers know, this takes a little practice. However, it is more fuel efficient to start from a stop then to reverse your direction when you're drifting backwards. With automatics, use the footbrake instead of the accelerator to hold your position when you're at an uphill stop sign or signal.

Build speed before climbing a hill.

By building up additional speed and momentum before you arrive at an uphill grade, you will reduce the need to shift down to a less efficient gear in which engine revolutions are higher and efficiency is lower.

The end of the climb.

If you charge over a peak, you'll have a lot of momentum, gravity will increase your speed even more on the way down the other side, and you'll be wasting gasoline by converting it into that infamous combination of friction heat and brake pad dust. Here's a better idea. Just prior to reaching the peak, save fuel by either shifting to a higher gear or lifting your right foot to encourage your automatic transmission to do so. By the time you reach the peak, you'll be going a little slower, the transmission will be in the higher gear, and your lower speed at the top will reduce the need for braking as you travel down the other side.

Let gravity be your friend.

If you're just starting down a steep hill, we hope you've followed our advice and topped the peak as slowly and safely as possible. Shift to the highest possible gear, either lift entirely from the accelerator or use an extremely light foot, and let gravity be your helper. If you're traversing through a series of climbs and descents, do the same thing at each opportunity. You'll save gas and engine wear because your car will always tend to be in the highest possible gear throughout the repeating sequence of ups and downs.

Hills: use air conditioning as another gear.

This is especially helpful to drivers of low-powered vehicles. In the 1980s and early 1990s, VW diesels with air conditioning and horsepower ratings of 52 hp or less really had ten speeds: five with the air conditioning on and five with the air conditioning off. It became second nature to turn off the air conditioning when climbing a hill and to turn it back on when descending. Although today's cars have a lot more horsepower, we can save fuel by using the same strategy. As you've probably noticed, the air conditioning cycles on and off—the compressor doesn't operate 100 percent of the time. You can save some fuel by turning the air conditioning either down or off on the way up a very steep grade, then turn it back on when you're descending the other side and gravity once again becomes your friend. On the way down, you will essentially be getting cooled off for free, because you've got the air conditioning cranked up and it is absorbing energy that would otherwise be wasted in braking.

Don't coast down hills.

This can be a tempting way to save fuel, but there are many reasons not to do it. First, it may be illegal. Second, if you have turned the engine off, you will have no power steering or power brakes. Third, with no drag resistance from the engine and little from the transmission, your brakes may overheat and fail. Fourth, automatic transmission internal components can overheat and be damaged because they are generating a lot of heat and receiving little or nothing in the way of cooling from an engine that is either shut off or idling. Fifth, if you make the mistake of removing the key from the ignition, the steering wheel lock will be activated and a very bad accident will quickly follow. There are many other ways to save fuel. Be sure to exclude this dangerous and possibly mechanically harmful temptation from your arsenal of strategies.

Sharing the road with large trucks.

There are two major rules here. Rule A: Think at least twice before you pass a large truck as it is starting down a long hill. After lumbering up the grade, the truck will almost surely accelerate to legal speeds and maybe beyond on the way down, and you will be left "hanging" out there in the passing lane. Your choices will then be to either drive very fast and inefficiently to overtake the truck or to back off and move in behind it—the latter possibility is the safer, more efficient, and much more preferable selection. Rule B: Stay out of their way. It's not a good idea to be macho when you're out there in the passing lane and all you can see behind you is the grille of a large truck. Move over, save fuel, and don't get upset.

When you're trailering or hauling.

If you're pulling a trailer or your vehicle is carrying a lot of passengers and/or weight, it becomes even more important to conserve momentum and avoid unnecessary braking. Smooth and steady speeds, staying further behind the vehicle in front, and extra vigilance in anticipating conditions ahead will help you get the best possible fuel economy.

A drag eraser.

Chances are your car is equipped with front disc brakes that work by pads being pushed into both sides of the rotating disc, or rotor. If you sometimes drive for long distances on a relatively straight road, this tip can reduce your rolling resistance. Disc brake pads, instead of fully retracting away from the rotor, will drag lightly against it after you've released the brake pedal. Your front wheel bearings, if adjusted properly, will have a very small amount of looseness, or "play." If you keep your foot off the brake, then very cautiously make a lane change or a left turn followed by a right turn, play in the wheel bearings can move the rotor just enough to push the brake pads very slightly away from the rotors. The result: less drag and more miles per gallon.

Is the parking brake really off?

A pull-up parking brake sometimes looks like it's all the way down, and the warning light may not be lit, but the brake might still be applied by just one click of the ratchet mechanism. Also, if someone is in the habit of using Herculean force in pulling up the parking brake lever, the cables going to the rear may become stretched and the handle could be raised just slightly even though the brakes are fully off. In any case, double-check by pressing the release button on the handle to make sure you're not wasting gas by forcing your engine to overcome the resistance of a slightly engaged parking brake.

Help your parking brake cables.

If you have drums instead of disc brakes at the rear, keep your foot on the brake pedal while you are applying the parking brake. In this way, the brake shoes will already be expanded against the drum and there will less stress on the parking brake cables and the conduits through which they run. By doing this, your parking brake cables will be less likely to fray, stretch, or "freeze up," and you can be more confident that your parking brakes are not wasting gas by trying to keep your car parked when you are telling it to go.

Reversing direction.

When you are traveling on a busy two-way road and discover that you're going the wrong way, there's a fuel efficient solution to your dilemma. Just drive a little further in the wrong direction, then turn left into a convenient parking lot. When you exit the lot, it will be easy and efficient for you to simply turn right and get into the traffic flow in the direction you wished to be traveling in the first place.

Making that difficult left turn.

You're at a stop sign and want to turn left onto a busy two-way road traveled by fast-moving drivers who don't have a stop sign. Instead of waiting for two lanes of busy traffic to become clear, save gas by just turning right instead, then follow the "reverse direction" tip that immediately precedes. Persistently waiting for two busy lanes to become clear at the same time may lead to a lengthy period during which you and your passenger will be playing the "It's-OK-to-the-left-what-about-the-right?" game and wasting precious gas.

Give space to turn signals.

If the vehicle you are following signals a turn, lift your foot from the accelerator and try to anticipate how soon he will be turning. By falling back just a bit, you can avoid wasteful braking when he actually slows and makes his turn, and you can resume your journey with minimal disruption to your momentum. Sometimes you can tell a driver is going to turn just by observing uncertain or bewildered behavior on his part. Fall back and give this driver extra space as well.

Turn right on red.

This practice not only helps keep traffic moving, it saves gas by avoiding unnecessary idling. Make sure it's legal before you do it, though!

Convert three rights into a left.

You'd like to turn left, but the lane for the left-turn traffic signal is extremely long. Perhaps there is not even a left-turn signal, and those wishing to turn left must rely on the generosity of drivers coming the other way. A fuel-efficient solution is to simply go straight through the intersection, turn right at the first opportunity, then turn right two more times. You will then be able to go through the intersection in the direction that you wanted in the first place. They say that two wrongs don't make a right, but we now know that three rights can make a left.

Arriving at the stop sign.

Avoid or minimize wasteful stop-and-go movements by timing your arrival at a stop sign so that nobody will be in front of you when you get there. Slow down early to minimize the number of vehicles (and position adjustments) that will be ahead of you.

Traffic signals: think "opposite."

When coming upon a traffic signal that's red, consider that it's likely to be green when you get there. When it's green, consider that it's likely to be red when you arrive. In either case, such intersections are no place to be driving fast, so save gas by lifting from the accelerator. If the light is likely to turn green, try to time your arrival so that you can continue through with minimal change in momentum. If the light is likely to turn red, approach even more slowly so you'll still be moving at least a little when it changes back to green.

Reading an intersection.

Upon approaching a signal-controlled intersection, take note of how many cars are in the centrally located turning lanes. If there are a lot of vehicles waiting, chances are they've been there for a while and the signal will soon be turning green. This is also true if there are a lot of vehicles waiting for the light to change and the volume of cross-traffic is sparse. As always, be efficient by lifting early from the accelerator, slowing with minimal braking, and not arriving at a traffic blockage any faster or sooner than necessary.

Managing a sequence of timed signals.

If a sequence of traffic signals is designed under the assumption that vehicles will be traveling 40 miles per hour between them, anyone traveling either faster or slower will encounter more red lights and use more fuel by having to make extra stops and starts. With a little practice, you can figure out the most efficient speed for dealing with such sequences on the routes you travel most often.

Don't charge a curve.

When approaching a sharp curve, lift from the accelerator early and slow down before reaching the part of the curve where your passengers would tend to get nervous. This minimizes both energy-wasting braking and unnecessary wear and tear on your passengers.

Exit ramp strategy.

First of all, be certain that you really want to take this exit. Changing your mind and attempting to return to the highway can be both inefficient and unsafe. If you are ready to exit, you are faced with the dilemma of maintaining a safe speed on the highway, then reducing to a lower speed that is safe for the curves of the exit ramp. Depending on the length of the "exit" lane, you may be able to lift your foot from the accelerator very early and minimize braking. Keep in mind that you'll probably have to stop at a sign or signal at the end of the ramp, so don't use any more fuel than necessary in arriving there.

Entrance ramp strategy.

When you're on the entrance ramp to a roadway where traffic is moving very quickly, the most important thing to do is to merge smoothly and safely. Any other behavior will waste fuel and be potentially dangerous. Anticipate openings in the traffic flow and try to blend in without disrupting your momentum, or that of the other cars.

Plan your exit before you park.

When parking at events where drivers will all be leaving at about the same time, either select the front half of a pull-through combo or (if it's legal) back into your parking space. It's easier and more efficient to pull forward into the exiting masses than to wait for someone kind enough to allow you to back out of your space. You'll save fuel and your blood pressure will thank you.

Turn off the air before you get there.

Don't waste fuel by running the air conditioning during those final few minutes before you arrive at your destination. The air already in the car will keep you comfortable during this short period of time.

The electric garage door opener.

This device not only enhances convenience and safety, it can also help you save just a bit of fuel. By pressing the "open" button prior to your arrival, you can continue your momentum and enter the garage without having to stop until you're inside. However, in your quest to maintain momentum, be sure the door has had time to fully open—otherwise, you could end up damaging the door or transforming your sedan into a convertible.

Read the wind.

Wind direction and velocity can greatly affect fuel efficiency, so it helps to have at least a rough idea of which way and how hard the wind is blowing. For clues, observe flags, chimney smoke, or falling leaves, and adjust your speed or your windows accordingly. For more details, see the next few tips.

Driving into the wind.

Driving into a strong wind is not the ideal condition for making up lost time. Keep in mind that air resistance is a function of how fast you're going relative to the air around you. If you're driving 60 miles per hour into a 20 mph headwind, your car will consume nearly as much fuel as it would if you were traveling 80 miles per hour on a calm day—and that's a lot of fuel.

Driving with the wind.

As with gravity, the wind can sometimes be our friend. If you're driving 60 miles per hour and being helped by a 20 mph tailwind, your car will experience the same air resistance as if you were driving only 40 miles per hour on a calm day. The result: a considerable improvement in fuel efficiency and an opportunity to make up some of that lost time. Or you can just drive at your normal speed and enjoy saving fuel. If you have a trip computer with mpg function, you'll see some incredible readings.

Driving through crosswinds.

The results may vary on this one. If there is a crosswind generally headed toward you, your fuel efficiency will decrease both because of the headwind effect and because your car will be less aerodynamic when moving through air that is coming at it from a sideward direction. If there is a crosswind generally heading in the same direction you're driving, you'll tend to get an improvement in fuel efficiency—however, this improvement will be less than if the wind were coming from directly behind you. If you're using the windows to assist with comfort and ventilation, slightly lower the windows on the side of the car opposite the direction from which the crosswind is coming. This will help decrease aerodynamic drag caused by in-car air turbulence, and fuel efficiency will be improved.

Use the trip computer to experiment.

If you have a trip computer that provides miles-per-gallon readings, use it to compare the results of different driving strategies over the same route, or to compare fuel efficiency with the windows down versus using air conditioning at various speeds and outside temperatures. By experimenting to find out what works best for you and your vehicle, you'll become more proficient at saving fuel. Be sure to reset the overall fuel consumption to zero prior to each of the alternatives involved in your experiment, and keep in mind that conditions from one test to the next should be as similar as possible so you'll have meaningful comparisons.

The trip computer challenge.

If you have a trip computer with the miles-per-gallon feature, have a contest in which you and your friends drive the same route and compare fuel consumption results. This can encourage the spirit of energy conservation and be a friendly way to compete. Try not to win all the time, or you may end up with fewer friends with whom to compete.

Pretend your odometer is a taxi fare meter.

This isn't too far-fetched, because each mile uses fuel, and fuel costs money. If you know the price per gallon and the approximate fuel economy your vehicle delivers, spending a few minutes with your pocket calculator will help you make this translation. If gas costs $4.00 per gallon and you're averaging 20 miles per gallon, each time the odometer racks up another 10 miles, you've just lost another two dollars. If that doesn't seem like much, wait until the gas gauge hits "E" and it's time for another $60 fill-up.

Be alert to your car's behavior.

Every once in a while, turn off the music and listen to the sounds your car is making. Even if you're not mechanically inclined, you may notice an irregularity that means something needs to be repaired or adjusted, and things that need repair or adjustment generally have a negative effect on fuel economy. Be especially conscious of your steering wheel and its position when you're traveling in a straight line, preferably on a flat road and on a calm day without crosswinds. For example, if the spokes were at the 9 o'clock and 3 o'clock positions yesterday and are now at clock positions two or more time zones away, there may have been a loss of pressure in one or both tires on one side of the car, or the front wheel alignment may have been disrupted by a pothole that didn't really seem very significant at the time.

CHAPTER 2

Fueling and Maintenance

Convert groceries into gas.

Get some of your gas money back by using promotional discounts and cash rebates that may be available at convenience stores, grocery stores, and other retailers that are not primarily in business to sell gasoline. They're just using the gasoline incentive to attract you to their store so you'll buy a lot of other things once you're inside—and, if they can make you a loyal customer, that's even better. See what cards or offers are available in your area or along the routes you travel, then save money by turning your groceries into discounts at the pump. As an example of these savings, participating Giant Eagle supermarkets in Pennsylvania have been offering a 1 percent discount on groceries for every 10 gallons of gas pumped at their gas-station partner.

Use oil company credit cards.

Give yourself a gas discount by using an oil company credit card and fueling at the company's stations. As with any credit card, carefully read the fine print and be sure to know how the system works. Try to use the card exclusively for gas purchases, and pay off the balance at the end of every month. Remember, the company is not doing this just because they like you, so do your homework and increase your knowledge before you commence to get discounts on your gas.

Don't overbuy octane.

Premium fuel has a premium price. When fueling up, buy only the octane level your car really needs. Check your owner's manual or the sticker on the fuel-filler door.

Winter gasoline contains less energy.

If you're keeping really close track of your gas mileage, keep in mind that winterized gasoline will tend to contain less energy. According to the Environmental Protection Agency, the average energy content of winter gasoline is 112,500 Btu (British thermal units) per gallon, compared to 114,500 Btu per gallon for its summer season counterpart. Because of the large number of other factors involved in the fuel economy you'll observe, chances are this 1.7 percent decrease in energy content will not be noticeable.

E10: be aware of ethanol blending.

Look for a gas pump sticker that shows how much of what you're pumping could be ethanol, an alcohol derived from corn and other agricultural products. Ethanol is admirable as a renewable resource, but it contains about 30 percent less energy per gallon than gasoline, so a mixture of the two will tend to slightly lower your fuel economy. When the mixture is 10 percent ethanol and 90 percent gasoline, this is known as gasohol, or E10. According to the Department of Energy, all vehicle manufacturers approve up to 10 percent ethanol in their gasoline engines. Nevertheless, lower energy content in the fuel blend tends to result in lower fuel economy. If the price at two stations is the same, opt for the one with the lower percentage of ethanol in the fuel.

Energy content may vary within a season.

Even within a given season, the energy content of gasoline can vary quite widely from batch to batch and from station to station. According to the Environmental Protection Agency, the energy content of a gallon of winter gasoline could be anywhere from 108,500 Btu to 114,000 Btu, with a gallon of summer gasoline containing between 113,000 Btu and 117,000 Btu.

Diesel fuel and antigel additives.

If you drive a diesel and live in a very cold climate, be sure the fuel you use is winterized and contains an additive to prevent it from taking on a jelly-like consistency that will inhibit flow and prevent starting in extremely cold temperatures. If you're not sure, buy your own fuel conditioner with antigel, but always follow the vehicle manufacturer's recommendations when you consider putting anything but fuel into the fuel tank.

Avoid the big "E."

Seeing the big "E" may be desirable when you're getting your vision checked at the optometrist's office, but it's not so good when you see it next to the pointer on your fuel gauge. By allowing the fuel level to get down to those last few pints, you may be inviting the fuel system to suck up all sorts of particles, debris, organisms, and other things that can clog things up and reduce efficiency.

Fill up in the morning.

Fuel will be more dense in the cooler morning temperatures, so you'll tend to get a little more energy content out of the volume you're buying. Although the storage tanks are a few feet underground and protect their contents from great temperature variations, they'll still be a little cooler after all those hours since the sun went down. If you're commuting, fill up on your way to work, not on your way home.

Pick the shady pump.

If you're not an early riser, you can still get some of that gas that's more cold and dense. If you happen to be out around midmorning, just select a station on the shady side of the street that hasn't seen the sun yet today.

Fill up before holidays and weekends.

The economic law of supply and demand suggests that you may find prices to be just a little better if you fill up a few days before the beginning of a holiday period or a weekend. It doesn't seem very often that we're greeted by lower gas prices at the beginning of the Memorial Day weekend, does it?

Avoid the crowd.

If possible, try to avoid crowded periods at the filling station. It's frustrating to waste gasoline while you're stuck in a stop-and-go line to get gasoline.

The dreaded tanker truck.

Avoid getting fuel when the fuel tanker truck is at the station. The process of filling up the underground storage tanks can stir up sediment that might otherwise have stayed at the bottom. Wait until things settle down.

Don't "top off" your tank.

Besides the money that's wasted when fuel overflows and spills out, topping off can be messy, and you, your car, and your trunk could smell like gasoline for awhile.

Use self-service.

If available in your state or locale, use self-service pumps. The gas may be cheaper, and you'll avoid the occasional station attendant who likes to continue pumping until the price reaches a round number, even if that means topping off your tank.

Get a full fill.

If you've either found a good price or you want to maximize your range before you have to pull off the interstate to refill, you'll want to really fill up when you fill up. If the area near the pump is uneven, position your vehicle so the filler opening is as high as possible. However, be sure to avoid wasting fuel by topping off the tank.

Turn off the engine while fueling.

Most filling stations have signs all over the place warning motorists about this practice, but it's not unusual to see people wasting fuel as well as risking life and limb while they complete their fill-up.

Pay at the pump.

If you've turned off the engine, as you should have, paying at the pump will enable you to leave much sooner and the engine will have had a little less time to cool down. Paying inside may require your standing in line behind someone buying twenty-five lottery tickets.

The foaming diesel.

With a diesel engine, it can be difficult to get an accurate reading on your fuel mileage. This is because the fuel foams up during filling. Depending on the vehicle, the tank might still be able to take another gallon or so after the pump nozzle has shut off. The trick is to allow the fuel to settle down for a minute or two before you put in the next gallon. For most people, this requires too much time and patience, but it's handy when you want to have a really full tank as you begin a long trip.

The elusive gas cap.

Don't forget to replace the gas cap, and make sure you turn it until it clicks. If you do forget it, either go back and pick it up or buy another one right away. Don't use a garage rag or washcloth as a long-term substitute—besides the danger, there will be excessive fuel loss from evaporation and the engine may not operate properly.

The gas cap gasket.

Every once in a while, check the rubber gasket on the gas cap to be sure it is not cracked and allowing gasoline to evaporate from the filler opening. Besides wasting fuel, a worn-out gasket can cause your car to fail emission tests, and some fuel systems are so sensitive that the "check engine" light may even come on if the gas cap gasket lacks the ability to seal.

Reset the odometer.

If you're keeping track of your fuel consumption, be sure to reset the trip odometer after you've filled the tank. If you don't, you'll lose a valuable source of information about your fuel economy—at least until you fill up the next time.

Fuel and clean.

When filling the tank, clean the windshield. You can't drive efficiently if you don't have a good view of your surroundings. If nobody's waiting, get the side windows, rear window, side mirrors, and lights as well. If you feel funny about doing this, just go through the car wash instead.

Fuel gauge translation.

Most fuel gauges just have an "E," an "F," and a red area you should avoid. There may also be miscellaneous markings between the extremes. With a little practice and experience, you can at least roughly translate the fuel gauge needle position into the number of gallons you have left. This tip is especially useful on long trips, and if you don't have a trip computer.

Use engine oil of the proper viscosity.

If you use oil with a higher viscosity than necessary, the oil will be too thick to properly lubricate the engine in cold weather. In addition, thicker oil will lead to more of what the engineers call "pumping loss," which means the engine will have to work harder and use more gasoline just to force the oil through the lubrication system. As always, follow your manufacturer's recommendations when making your oil selection. According to the U.S. Department of Energy, using the thicker SAE 10W-30 in an engine designed to use SAE 5W-30 can reduce your fuel economy by one to two percent. Note that "SAE" stands for the Society of Automotive Engineers, while 5 and 30 represent the viscosity range of the oil. The higher the numbers, the thicker the oil.

Look for the "Energy-Conserving" oil label.

Be sure to use an engine oil that is designated as "Energy Conserving" on the label. These oils have additional friction-reducing additives that will make the oil even more slippery and further improve your vehicle's fuel efficiency.

Synthetic oil and lubricants.

If they fall within your manufacturer's recommendations, seriously consider synthetic oils and lubricants for both fuel efficiency and oil performance. These are not petroleum-based and they will be more expensive, but they will be very effective in withstanding extreme temperatures and operating conditions.

Change engine oil and filter regularly.

Change your engine oil and filter at least as frequently as the manufacturer recommends. Oil not only lubricates the moving parts of the engine, it also carries away heat and, by means of the oil filter, removes metallic and other particles from the lubrication system. However, during its lifetime, the oil inevitably picks up chemical contaminants and its additives lose effectiveness. Deterioration and contamination of the engine oil will be especially severe if most of your trips are very short and involve a lot of cold starts. Regular oil and filter changes are one of the best forms of insurance for the life and fuel efficiency of your engine. If you have your oil changed by somebody other than the vehicle dealer, keep detailed receipts and make sure you've satisfied your obligations under the vehicle warranty agreement.

Changing it yourself.

If you're a do-it-yourselfer who changes your own engine oil and filter, there are a number of things to take into consideration. If the vehicle is still under warranty, be sure that the dealer approves and that by performing your own oil changes you won't cause the warranty to become void. Be sure to use the manufacturer-specified type and viscosity of oil, and don't forget to keep detailed receipts for your oil and filter purchases. Even if the vehicle is no longer under warranty, you should still use the type and viscosity of oil that has been specified by the manufacturer. After you're done, be a friend to the environment and properly recycle the used oil.

Maintain the proper oil level.

Check the engine oil level frequently and try to maintain it at the "full" level on the dipstick. To get a more accurate measurement, wait a minute or two after shutting off the car to allow oil that has been circulating some time to gravitate back down to the crankcase.

Keep a maintenance log.

Regardless of who does the oil and filter changes or other work on your vehicle, keep a detailed record of dates, mileages, and descriptions of what was done. This applies whether your car is new or old, under warranty or not—it's simply a good idea, and your car deserves better than relying on the "next service due . . ." sticker on the windshield. Keep receipts for any maintenance or repair work. This will enhance the resale value of your vehicle. Regular maintenance helps your older car have the dependability of a much younger one, and this is an important factor for the majority of us who own cars that aren't exactly fresh from the showroom. According to R.L. Polk & Co., the median age of U.S. cars is 9.4 years, and 41 percent of our cars are at least 11 years old.

Keep your tires properly inflated.

Underinflated tires are dangerous and inefficient, and their increased rolling resistance can greatly reduce your fuel economy. According to the U.S. Department of Energy, when all four tires are underinflated, fuel economy will be reduced by 0.3 percent for each pound of underinflation. Thus, if your tires are all underinflated by 10 pounds, your fuel economy will be reduced by 3 percent. Check your tires at least as often as your vehicle manufacturer recommends, and check them when they are cold. Be especially vigilant if you're driving an older car with alloy wheels, as the wheel surface tends to oxidize and leave a powdery residue. This makes proper sealing a challenge for many tire shops. Tire pressure recommendations can be found in your owner's manual, or on a sticker on the trunk lid, doors, or door frames.

Buy a gauge and tire pump.

For best results, buy an accurate tire pressure gauge and a high-volume bicycle pump. Keep them handy and check the pressures frequently. The gauges at gas stations and convenience stores are not known for accuracy. If you've just purchased new tires, be sure to check their pressures as soon as you get home and the tires have had a chance to cool down overnight.

Don't eyeball tire pressure.

Don't simply walk around the car and conclude that all the tires look okay. The sidewalls of radial tires always bulge a little, but if they happen to be bulged a little more than usual, it's difficult to detect this visually and translate it into a solid tire pressure estimate. Don't rely on visual inspection—use an accurate gauge and use it often.

Don't forget the spare.

When you're checking the tire pressures, don't forget to check the spare tire every third time or so. Its location is generally not very convenient, but don't be tempted to put off the check. Note that some space-saving tires require higher air pressure than regular tires. A spare's pressure recommendation will typically be found on a sticker on the trunk lid or a notice on the sidewall or wheel of the tire.

Tire pressures and temperature changes.

It was an unusually warm and balmy 80 degrees yesterday, but a weather front has arrived and it's going to be no higher than 50 degrees for the next week or so. If your tires were properly inflated yesterday, they are not properly inflated today. As the temperature decreased, the pressure within the tires also decreased. Thanks to a 30-degree drop in temperature, you will probably need to add at least a few pounds of pressure to each tire.

Get clues from your tires.

Check your tires for flat spots and uneven wear patterns. These can indicate a number of possible problems that can impact fuel efficiency, including out-of-balance wheels, weak shock absorbers, improper wheel alignment, or tires that have had too much or too little air pressure for a long time.

Clean up the treads.

When examining your tires, remove stones and other objects from the tread area. Besides increasing rolling resistance, they could get forced through the tread and puncture the tire. Such damage is especially likely if the tires have been in use for many miles and the tread is relatively thin. If you've recently spilled a box of roofing nails in your garage, be especially observant.

Rotate your tires.

If the vehicle manufacturer recommends it, have your tires rotated according to the suggested pattern. This can help your tires last longer, wear more evenly, and better retain their low rolling resistance. Keep in mind that some tires have "unidirectional" construction or tread design, meaning that they should rotate in the direction of the arrow on the sidewall whenever the car is moving forward. Such tires should not be switched from the right side of the car to the left, or vice-versa.

Balance the wheels.

Poorly balanced wheels will reduce fuel efficiency in the short run and increase the need for vehicular repairs in the long term. Tires that shake and hop at highway speeds will skip and develop flat spots, causing extra wear on suspension components.

Check plastic wheel covers.

Because they are generally quite fragile, the plastic wheel covers used on many steel wheels should be examined carefully to ensure the integrity of their mounting hardware and plastic tabs. Broken mounting tabs can cause a wheel cover to be off-center on its wheel, and the $10 wheel balance you just paid for will be wasted when the off-center cover is installed and you head down the road.

Remove the wheel covers at home.

Tire shops generally post a warning that they are not responsible for hubcaps and wheel covers once you leave the premises. Because of their fragility, remove those plastic wheel covers yourself before you go for wheel balancing or tire replacement. If those covers get damaged, it could negate the positive effects of any work your mechanic has done and reduce fuel efficiency.

Front-end alignment.

The tires at the front of your car will have less rolling resistance if they are both trying to roll in the same direction. When they try to go in different directions, sideward dragging occurs and that means excessive tire wear and fuel consumption. Wheels that are aimed towards the same point down the road will be slightly "pigeon-toed," a condition referred to as "toe-in." Wheels that would move farther apart if they were to leave the car have a condition known as "toe-out." The amount of toe-in or toe-out is one of the most important specifications involving the direction and orientation of the wheels. According the U.S. Environmental Protection Agency, front wheels that are badly out of alignment can reduce fuel economy by as much as 10 percent.

Four-wheel alignment.

Rear-wheel alignment can have an effect on fuel economy because these are the wheels that determine the natural direction in which the car tends to move. The front wheels simply allow you to go in the direction *you* choose. As with the front wheels, misaligned rear wheels can reduce fuel economy, and some manufacturers may recommend a four-wheel alignment instead of just attending to the fronts.

Camber counts.

Tires roll more easily when they're relatively perpendicular to the road surface. Depending on the vehicle and the manufacturer's specifications for best handling and steering, the wheels might require slight positive camber (the tire leans a little outward, away from the vehicle) or negative camber (the tire leans slightly inward, towards the vehicle.) Specifications often call for each of the front wheels to have the same amount of camber, often positive, and for each of the rear wheels to have the same as well, often negative. Regardless of front or rear, rolling resistance will increase and fuel economy will go down if there is too much camber in either direction.

Don't "reverse" your wheels.

Sometimes people reverse their wheels (turn them around so the sides that are supposed to face the car now face away.) They do this to increase the width of the track or in hopes of improving handling or appearance. This is a bad idea for two reasons: First, this will usually increase the negative camber by moving the wheels farther away from the car and forcing them to lean in a little more to support its weight. Second, the more outward location of the wheel and tire can put extra stress on the wheel bearings. Among the end results are increased rolling resistance and lower fuel economy.

The "hands off" test.

While driving on a flat road on a calm day, very slightly remove your hands from the steering wheel for just a moment. Does the car continue traveling in a straight line? If not, it's possible the camber of the wheels on one side of the car might not match that of their counterparts on the other side of the car. If that's the case, the car will tend to drift toward the same side of the road as the front tire that has the more positive camber. There can be many other possible causes for this drifting, including improperly inflated tires, dragging brakes, other alignment issues, or even a broken crossways belt in a steel-belted radial tire. No matter what the cause, if you are drifting to one side, you're probably fuel-inefficient. Get the problem diagnosed and fixed as soon as possible.

Fuel-efficient replacement tires.

Don't skimp when buying tires. Replacement tires could have as much as 50 percent greater rolling resistance than the ones installed when your car was new. To help meet federal fuel efficiency standards, automakers typically install more efficient tires than the ones most people buy as replacements. Select replacement tires of comparable quality to the originals, especially in regard to tread-wear rating. The higher the tread-wear rating, the more miles your tires will travel before wearing out, and this is a good indicator of low rolling resistance. According to Green Seal Environmental Partners, an independent nonprofit organization, our national fuel economy would be 3 percent higher if all replacement tires were as efficient as the originals. One of the biggest promoters of fuel-efficient tires is Michelin, whose engineers claim up to 8 percent greater fuel efficiency for their most efficient tire compared to standard designs. They also equate use of this tire model to planting forty trees, as less rolling resistance means less carbon dioxide produced in the exhaust, and a single mature tree can absorb up to 48 pounds of carbon dioxide a year. It's an unusual analogy, but another good argument for saving fuel. To help tire buyers get the most fuel-efficient tires for their money, the National Highway Traffic Safety Administration proposed in 2009 that tires be labeled for rolling resistance and fuel efficiency, as well as for the current labels that provide safety and tread life estimates. Low rolling resistance is the gold standard by which the fuel efficiency of tires is measured— e.g., Goodyear says its new Assurance Fuel Max tire has 27 percent less rolling resistance than conventional tires.

Replacement tires: buy the same size.

When your original tires wear out, be sure to replace them with tires that are the same size as those that came with the car when it was new. With other design and construction factors the same, replacements that are lower-profile and wider than the originals will have greater rolling resistance and result in lower fuel economy.

Don't forget new valve stems.

If you've been making the effort to periodically inflate your tires to the correct pressure, take steps to make sure the air stays where you put it. When you get those replacement tires, be sure to buy new valve stems as well, and make sure they're the right length. If they're too short, you may have difficulty reaching them for inflation checks; if they're too long, they'll stick out too far and look funny.

Put your best wheels forward.

Generally speaking, you should put your best wheels in front, because even a small amount of run-out or wiggle in the rotation of a front wheel will be more noticeable and annoying than in the rotation of a rear wheel. Also, the front end of the car will likely be heavier than the rear, so if you put the best wheels up front, you'll help minimize the effects that imperfections have on rolling resistance and fuel economy. One way to find out which two wheels are best is to have a tire shop identify them for you the next time you get your wheels balanced.

Don't over-tighten wheel nuts or bolts.

The owner's manual will typically include tightness specifications for the wheel nuts or bolts. If these are not tight enough, the wheel could come off. If they are severely over-tightened, they can warp the shape of the brake rotor (disc brakes) or the brake drum (drum brakes). This can lead to uneven braking and tire wear, greater rolling resistance, and lower fuel economy.

Check the battery terminals.

With your engine off, check for powdery corrosion at the battery terminals, especially the one on the positive (+) side. This acidic corrosion reduces the efficiency of your battery, and that wastes gas. After you or your mechanic has carefully removed the corrosion with a mixture of baking soda and water, dry and grease the terminals. You may need to disconnect one of the terminals, maybe both, so be sure to follow the manufacturer's instructions with regard to jotting down things like radio antitheft code numbers before you start.

Replace a weak battery.

If your starter is no longer turning the engine at its usual speed, and if your battery is at or beyond the higher end of its warranteed lifetime, get a new battery. Don't waste the fuel it takes for the engine and charging system to continue trying to feed electricity to a battery that can no longer hold it.

Replacement battery: get the standard.

Unless you really need the extra starting capacity, buy the standard battery instead of an optional one that is larger and heavier.

Batteries contain lead plates, lead is heavy, and extra weight requires extra gas.

Follow the maintenance schedule.

Read the maintenance chapter of your owner's manual and be sure to follow it rigorously. This includes minor and major tune-ups according to scheduled mileage or time intervals. According to the U.S. Federal Trade Commission, regularly scheduled tune-ups can increase fuel economy by an average of 4 percent.

Read a technical manual.

To better appreciate your vehicle's components and complexities, buy a repair and maintenance manual. Even an inexpensive guide will help you decide what you can and should do, and what you should have done by a professional. Even if you don't do any of your own work, knowing more about your car will help you identify fuel-robbing irregularities and to better communicate with your mechanic. Also, if you're traveling and you have car problems away from home, your added knowledge might save you from being taken advantage of by someone who happens to be less honest than your local mechanic.

Don't ignore the "Check Engine" light.

The light is bright, it's annoying, and it stays on constantly even though your car seems to be running fine. But that light came on for a reason, and chances are that reason is affecting how efficiently your engine is running. Read the owner's manual to see if attention is required right now, or just soon. If the answer is "soon," don't just stick electrical tape over the light—make an appointment with the mechanic to find out what's going on.

Know when to shut down.

A blinking "Check Engine" light should never be ignored, as it may be trying to tell you that something is very wrong and that you should pull over and shut down as soon and safely as possible. As always, read the owner's manual or ask your mechanic what is being communicated by various warning light modes. If your engine is sending you a frantic S.O.S., you are undoubtedly fuel inefficient, but that may be the least of your worries.

Check the fluids.

One of the easiest and most important things you can do to maintain efficiency is to open the hood and check the levels of vital fluids and lubricants, especially engine coolant, engine oil, and power steering fluid. (Note: never remove the coolant cap when your engine is hot, as the coolant will be under pressure as well as being extremely hot.) Although it's a little less vital, this is a good time to top up the windshield washer fluid. If you have automatic transmission, checking levels and topping them off is a little more complex. In any case, exercise caution and follow the instructions and precautions in the owner's manual.

Belt checks.

Either you or your mechanic should occasionally examine the accessory drive belts to be sure they are not cracked or frayed, and that they are neither too loose nor too tight. Loose belts will slip, causing the accessories they drive to work improperly. Loose belts will fail relatively quickly as well. Overly tight belts put extra strain on the bearings of the accessories they drive, shortening their lives as well as the life of the belt. Whether a belt is too loose or too tight, both fuel economy and the economy of ownership will suffer.

What did I touch?

Whether you've just checked the engine oil level or spent all day replacing the camshaft timing belt, there is one thing you should always ask yourself before you close the hood, and that is, "What did I touch while I was in here?" Even the most meticulous owner has occasionally forgotten to replace the oil filler cap after topping off the engine oil level, and even the most careful mechanic has sometimes left a wrench or two behind. A quick look around can help prevent damage and lost fuel efficiency.

What did they touch?

If you want your vehicle to run efficiently, you'll need to rely on repair shops and dealers to perform operations you either can't or don't want to tackle. If you're skeptical about whether someone will actually do what you ask, you can carefully and discreetly mark some of the parts that should be affected by the procedures. For example, if you pay for a new fuel filter, you can mark your current one to make sure it isn't shined up and passed off as new. This needn't take on the complexity of a James Bond secret agent operation, but consider it self-protection against the occasionally unscrupulous shop or dealer.

Replace the fuel filter.

If it is not replaced at the recommended intervals, the fuel filter may become clogged. This will place an extra burden on the electric fuel pump, reduce the efficiency with which the engine receives and utilizes fuel, and cause a decrease in fuel economy.

Diesels: check the water separator.

Some diesel-powered vehicles might contain a water separator within the fuel filter itself and/or an auxiliary water separator in the fuel supply system. The purpose of this device is to rid the fuel of any water that might have found its way into the system, perhaps by condensation within the fuel tank. Follow the manufacturer's instructions when draining or replacing the separator. Diesel fuel injectors are made to incredibly precise tolerances, and in order for them to operate efficiently, it is essential that they be free both from moisture that could lead to corrosion and various contaminants that could lead to clogging.

Change the engine air filter.

Don't give your engine asthma by driving around with a dirty air filter. Change the filter at least as often as the vehicle manufacturer recommends. Every gallon of gas requires about 10,000 gallons of air, and replacing a dirty or clogged air filter can help keep your engine running properly and efficiently.

Don't forget the cabin air filter.

Many cars have a cabin air filter through which outside air passes before it enters the ventilation ductwork and then the car. These filters are typically more expensive than regular engine air filters, but they nevertheless should be replaced at the recommended intervals. If they become dirty or clogged, the resistance to air flow will increase, causing the ventilation fan to work harder. This requires more power, which in turn will reduce fuel economy.

Intake air diversion thermostat.

Some cars have a thermostatically controlled device that, when the engine is cold, draws engine intake air from a hot area near the exhaust manifold rather than from outside the car. This helps reduce emissions and improves performance when the engine is cold. Once the engine is warm, this device allows the engine to draw cooler air from outside. If the thermostat or related parts fail, the engine could draw in hot air all of the time, even at highway speeds in high temperatures. A steady diet of such heated air could damage some expensive components within the air intake system of a fuel-injected engine. If your vehicle has one of these devices, be sure your mechanic checks to make sure it is working properly. Failing to check a single, inexpensive device can flatten both your fuel economy and your wallet.

Replace the PCV valve.

The PCV (positive crankcase ventilation) valve is an emissions-control device that's been around for a very long time, and it allows unburned combustion gases and fumes within the crankcase to return to the intake system for reburning. Most tune-ups include cleaning or replacing this part. If the PCV valve gets clogged or fails, the engine will idle poorly and inefficiently, and pressure can build up, resulting in leaking gaskets and seals. This device is good for the environment and for your engine's life and efficiency, so be sure it gets the attention it needs.

Replace the spark plugs.

In gasoline engines, the spark plugs provide a high-voltage zap to the fuel-air mixture, causing an explosion that produces power. If a spark plug is worn or has an excessive gap between its electrodes, the electrical jolt will be weaker, and engine power and fuel efficiency will suffer. In modern ignition systems, spark plugs don't have to be replaced as often as they used to, but be sure they are checked and/or changed at the recommended intervals. According to the EPA, a single misfiring spark plug can lower your gas mileage by up to 4 percent. If yours is one of the many vehicles with an engine compartment so crowded that you can't even find the spark plugs, this is a job best left to the mechanic.

Looking for electricity leaks.

If the engine in your older car has been running a little rough lately and your gas mileage is down, it's possible that those old ignition wires might have some cracks and are transmitting some of their electricity to each other instead of to the spark plugs. Locate the distributor and the ignition wires, then turn out the lights. With the hood open, the engine idling, and you standing at a safe distance, look for any flashes of electricity. If you notice some wires that seem to be sending electricity to each other or to a metal part of the engine, it may be time for a fresh set of ignition wires that will restore your engine's fuel efficiency.

The engine-driven cooling fan.

Using a conventional fan belt, this device draws air through the radiator to cool the engine, but it also uses energy and is not really necessary when you're traveling at highway speeds and there is already plenty of outside air being pushed through the radiator. If you have this type of cooling fan, you are wasting power, but you can take some comfort in the fact that it's likely to have a viscous hub that allows it to "coast" when the engine is warm. Ask your dealer or mechanic about permanent solutions to this problem, but know that depending on the age of your car, you might just have to live with this arrangement until you get a newer vehicle with a thermostatically controlled electric fan that only works when it's needed. In the meantime, you can at least minimize its effect on your fuel economy by keeping the blades spotlessly clean so they'll move through the air as efficiently as possible.

If the temperature gauge always says "C."

After you've driven several miles or so, the coolant temperature gauge should move toward the center portion of the scale. If the gauge still indicates "C" (for cold, of course) after you know the engine should be warmed up, it's possible the cooling system thermostat is stuck in the "open" position, thus allowing too much coolant to flow through the radiator. If this is the case, the result will be a cold-running engine to which the engine management computer may continue to feed a rich and inefficient fuel-air mixture. Have your mechanic look into this matter and, if necessary, replace the coolant thermostat with a new one. They're very cheap compared to the gas you'd otherwise be wasting.

If the temperature gauge always says "H."

If the coolant temperature gauge always ends up at the "H" (hot) end of the scale, the coolant thermostat may be stuck in the "closed" position and preventing coolant from circulating and cooling the engine. This is a serious condition—do not put off a trip to the mechanic. Poor fuel economy is the least of your problems, since you could end up with an overheated and badly damaged engine.

Check exhaust system integrity.

Encounters with road debris can sometimes cause unwanted dents or kinks in the pipes of your exhaust system. This can inhibit the system's performance by constricting exhaust flow and reducing fuel efficiency. If you've recently run over a fallen-off truck tread or some other object on the road, be sure to include the exhaust system among the under-vehicle components you check for damage.

The incredibly giant exhaust pipe.

We've all seen a modified car with an exhaust pipe that seems to have the diameter of a grapefruit. This can improve flow through the system, but be sure you and your mechanic know what you're doing, and that modifications are in compliance with noise, emission, and other legal requirements.

Air conditioning checks.

Have the system examined periodically to make sure it's working efficiently, that there are no air bubbles visible in the system's sight glass, and that the compressor is not wasting fuel and energy by circulating a refrigerant charge that's too great or too little. If you live in a warm climate, you'll be rewarded with maximum comfort at a minimum cost to your fuel budget.

Those zillion vacuum hoses.

In today's engines, there are vacuum hoses galore, and almost nobody seems to know what they all do. If you're experiencing some engine roughness and your gas mileage is down, you might want to take a look at each end of as many vacuum hoses as you can conveniently see. Both ends should be attached to something. If you've recently had work done on your vehicle, the mechanic may have accidentally detached one or both ends of a hose. If you're not sure how or where to attach a hose, consult your manual or mechanic. This might not be a sure-thing solution to your gas mileage problem, but its ease and zero cost make it worth at least a token attempt.

Don't tamper.

It's not a good idea to tinker with today's complicated and electronically controlled engines in an attempt to get more performance or efficiency. If you don't know what you're doing, you could end up with a poorly running, less efficient engine. Even if you do know what you're doing, you could tamper your way right past legal limits or government-imposed standards.

Clutch free play.

This sounds like a playground game, but it's important if you drive a manual transmission. The manufacturer will generally specify a free play distance through which the clutch pedal should move before it actually begins to disengage the engine from the transmission. Too little free play can lead to clutch wear and slippage, and to reduced fuel economy. If there is too much free play, the engine and transmission may not fully disengage when you press the clutch pedal, and shifting may be difficult. If you have too much free play, it's also possible your cruise control will either shut off unexpectedly or not work at all—in this case, the clutch pedal is riding too low and not closing the adjacent switch that's responsible for shutting off the cruise control when you shift gears.

Time for a new clutch?

If you stop on the way up a steep hill, you should be able to engage the clutch and proceed up the hill. If the clutch continues slipping after you release the pedal, that's a bad sign. In this event, chances are that you have little or no free play at the clutch pedal, or the clutch linings are worn and you'll need a whole new clutch.

Do a visual check of coolant hoses.

A visual examination of the coolant hoses can reveal bulges, cracks, kinking, fraying, and failure that could lead to coolant loss and expensive engine damage. Damaged coolant hoses can also reduce your fuel efficiency by making your engine work harder and use more gasoline to pump the coolant through the system.

Check the coolant cap.

When the engine and coolant are cold, remove the cap from the coolant overflow container and check the gasket. If it is cracked or broken, it is not properly pressurizing the coolant when the engine warms up and the coolant expands. If the coolant is not pressurized, it will have a lower boiling point. Also, it may contain tiny air bubbles that are either stirred up by motion of the water pump blades or caused by the general stirring that takes place during coolant circulation. This is referred to as "cavitation," and it can reduce the efficiency of the cooling system, affecting your engine's operating temperature and fuel efficiency. Coolant caps are cheap but very important. When replacing yours, be sure to get one that is rated at the same pressurization level (pounds per square inch) as the original.

Replace the coolant.

Many people ignore the fact that engine coolant deteriorates over the miles and its protective additives and lubrication qualities become depleted. A quality coolant that flows more easily will contribute to better fuel economy, so change it at the recommended intervals. Be sure to follow the vehicle manufacturer's recommendations when selecting replacement coolant and, whoever performs the replacement, try to ensure that the old coolant is properly recycled.

Clean the radiator surface.

Help maintain the effectiveness of the cooling system by clearing the radiator of airflow inhibitors such as leaves, candy wrappers, road debris, and bugs. The result will be more efficient cooling and better fuel economy.

Clean the condenser.

If you have air conditioning, one of its components will be a radiator-like structure (the condenser) that is usually mounted in front of the radiator. An occasional cleaning of the condenser will improve air conditioning efficiency and boost your car's fuel economy.

The straight braking test.

If your car does not drift toward either side of a flat road while driving, but veers to one side or the other when you apply the brakes, chances are one or more of your brakes is dragging or not releasing fully. This leads to lower fuel economy, so get them checked soon.

Pay attention to your brakes.

If your brakes make squealing or grinding noises, if the car slows down unevenly, or if the brake pedal pulsates when you press it, have the brakes closely examined. With disc brakes, a grinding noise may be caused by metal-on-metal contact resulting from worn pads. In disc brakes, uneven braking and a pulsating pedal suggest that one or more of the rotors is warped—i.e., the rotor is not of equal thickness all the way around. With drum brakes, the same uneven braking and pulsation can occur when the brake drums are out of round. Have the brakes examined by a professional. When driving efficiently, you do practically everything you can to avoid using the brakes, so don't let them slow you down when you don't want them to.

Do your brake calipers really float?

All disc brakes have a caliper that positions the brake pads on both sides of the rotor. In most of today's calipers, just one side of the caliper contains the piston(s) that push against the brake pad on that side. The brake pad on the other side is fixed in place, and equal force from the two sides occurs as the caliper "floats" on sideways pins. The caliper's ability to float back and forth compensates for wear as the pads become thinner. This is how it's supposed to happen, but the floating-caliper pins are subject to wear and corrosion, and must be serviced or replaced according to the manufacturer's recommendations. If the floating-caliper pins are not doing their job, the caliper will not float and the brake pads may not fully release from the rotor when you take your foot off the brake. The result will be uneven brake pad wear, dragging brakes, and lower fuel economy.

Spin your wheels.

Suggest to your mechanic that he put your car on a lift, apply the brakes and release them, then spin each of the wheels by hand to see how easily it moves. Of course, he will need to take into consideration that the driving wheels (the ones connected to the transmission) will require a little more force. If one or more of the wheels is extremely difficult to rotate, you might need new pads, rotors, brake shoes, or drums. But this simple first step is a great indicator of potential problems.

The at-home "push test" for brakes.

If you have a garage with a flat floor, have a friend place the car in neutral, turn off the engine, and release the handbrake. Then, possibly with the help of another friend, get a grip on the bumper and push the car. Unless the vehicle is extremely heavy and has tires with high rolling resistance, you shouldn't have much trouble getting the car rolling. If the car moves easily, this is a good sign, but be safe by making sure your driver-seat friend is alert and ready to apply the parking brake or press heavily on the brake pedal. If the car strongly resists movement, the brakes could be dragging badly or failing to release when the brake pedal is released. Either way, you could be wasting gas, so it could be time to visit the mechanic.

Safety inspections and rear drum brakes.

When a state safety inspection is performed on disk brakes, the inspector need only remove the wheel to inspect the condition of the rotor and braking pads. But on cars with rear drum brakes, the entire brake drum may also have to be removed. This means removing the outer wheel bearing, the retaining nut and washer, the retaining nut cover, and the cotter pin as well. After the inspection they must be reinstalled (with a new cotter pin) and the rear wheel bearings must be properly adjusted. Make sure your mechanic double-checks that the rear wheels move freely. Bearings that are well greased and properly adjusted minimize rolling resistance, so don't let a state inspection come between you and higher fuel economy.

Replace the brake fluid.

Brake fluid absorbs water, and water is more dense than brake fluid, so any moisture in your braking system will find its way to a caliper (disk brake) or a wheel cylinder (drum brake.) This can lead to corrosion and failure of the parts involved, which is why manufacturers recommend that the brake fluid be replaced at specified intervals. This process may involve bleeding the brakes to purge foreign matter and bubbles from the hydraulic system, and a professional is the best choice for this job. Remember that deficient brakes will contribute to deficient fuel economy.

Check the CV boots.

Cars with front-wheel drive have four constant velocity joints, the purpose of which is to transmit torque smoothly from the transmission drive shafts to the driving wheels. Some vehicles also have these joints at the rear, especially if the rear wheels also help to propel the car. Periodically check the integrity of the rubber boots on these joints. If a boot is cracked or torn, moisture will quickly enter the system, and the joint will begin making loud clicking noises, especially when you turn or accelerate. Don't try to nurse along a joint that is making such noises—it's going to get even worse very soon. Besides presenting possible dangers, its greater drag will be wasting fuel as you witness its deterioration.

Maintain an aerodynamic exterior.

During a typical NASCAR race, cars bang into each other and their pit crews use a lot of effort and duct tape to hold things together and help the cars' bodies stay relatively streamlined. Although we bump into each other less frequently, dents or other body damage can increase your car's air resistance at highway speeds. For example, panels, fenders, or bumpers may stick out slightly as the result of a parking lot incident. Even if you don't plan on having such items immediately repaired by a professional, you may wish to at least push or bend them back closer to where they used to be. You will still not have the sleekest vehicle on the planet, but your fuel economy will be a little better.

The front bumper air deflector.

Many cars have at least a small air deflector beneath the front bumper. Besides helping cooling air to enter the engine compartment, this device also makes the car more aerodynamic by directing oncoming air around the car instead of beneath it. These deflectors are easily damaged, especially when you pull too far forward and scrape the concrete barrier at the front of a parking space. If necessary, patch and reinforce it with flat pieces of thin plastic cut from an oil container (try to find one that's the same color as the deflector). Use pop rivets or narrow plastic tie wraps to secure the pieces in place. It might not look as nice as when it was new, but your car will now be slightly more aerodynamic and fuel efficient.

Check underbody panels.

There is likely a plastic panel beneath at least part of your engine. It serves a variety of purposes, including reducing air turbulence beneath the vehicle, protecting engine and steering components from slush and road-debris damage, and assisting the flow of cooling air through the engine compartment. Damage to the panel can inhibit its protective and aerodynamic functions. Removing and patching a damaged panel can lower air resistance and improve fuel economy.

Wash and wax.

By occasionally washing and waxing your car, you can help make its surface a little more slippery and less resistant to the air through which you're driving. In this case, beauty is more than skin deep—it reaches the fuel tank as well.

CHAPTER 3

Planning

Take the bus or subway instead.

If you're not driving your car, it can't use any gas. Taking the bus, subway, or some alternative form of public transportation will save you gas. As a bonus, you'll also avoid traffic headaches, parking expenses, and other worries.

Walk, jog, or bike.

It's simple, but it works. You'll improve your health and, besides spending less on gas, you can save even more money by dropping your membership at the fitness club. If you're thinking about moving, check *www.walkscore.com*, where you can type in an address and get a "walkability" index based on the variety of things you can get to by walking a mile or less.

Is anybody out there?

If you are planning to run out on some minor errand but know that somebody in your household is already on the road or will be returning soon from work or play, call and ask her to make a stop on her way home. She won't mind, and you'll save the expense of an unnecessary and fuel-thirsty short trip.

Stay off the roof.

Don't put luggage and other gear on the roof unless there is absolutely no alternative. Rummage on the roof increases your car's air resistance and dramatically reduces your highway fuel economy. If you must use a rooftop carrier, make sure it's level, secure, and as rearward as safety considerations allow. According to the U.S. Department of Energy, a rooftop carrier can decrease fuel efficiency by as much as 5 percent. This is conservative, and aerodynamic subcompacts with a large rooftop carrier can expect a much greater penalty.

When you must use the roof.

If you have no choice but to place items on the roof and you do not have a rooftop carrier, try to minimize the aerodynamic drag by placing smaller items in front and larger items towards the rear. If your vehicle has permanent bars at the sides of the roof, be sure to remove the perpendicular carrier bars when they're not in use.

Roof-topping a kayak or small boat.

If you're strapping a kayak or small boat to the roof, be sure to place the more streamlined end forward and position the craft as far back as safety considerations permit. Also, try to pull the front of the craft as close to the roof as possible to reduce the amount of oncoming air that will get underneath it. If you have a van, wagon, crossover, or SUV, rearward placement will be especially effective, because you can move the boat farther to the rear than with a sedan.

Rooftop carriers: the good news.

Keeping the roof clear will be always be more fuel efficient than placing carriers or anything else up there. On the other hand, if owning a removable rooftop carrier allows you to get by with a smaller vehicle, then the everyday savings you enjoy will far outweigh the extra gas consumed by occasional use of the rooftop carrier.

Rent or borrow a small trailer.

There are times when you need a vehicle bigger than your small, efficient car. Instead of renting a big gas-guzzler, consider renting or borrowing a small trailer. Because it will be "drafting" very closely behind the car, its effect on your car's aerodynamics and fuel efficiency will be much less than you'd think. Be sure to follow your vehicle manufacturer's recommendations regarding trailer use, including permissible trailer and hitch weights.

The least efficient trip of all.

Generally speaking, the worst trip of all is the one you make to buy nothing but a tank of gas. However, there can be some logical exceptions. In most cases, you could have made the gas purchase while running some other errands.

Think fuel, not distance.

Think in terms of fuel consumed, not distance traveled, and try to select routes that have fewer stop signs and traffic signals, and less traffic congestion. Taking a slightly longer route can sometimes be advantageous if it allows you to drive more efficiently.

Avoid peak travel and shopping times.

Whenever possible, plan to drive when traffic will be lighter. Driving will be more efficient, and you'll be able to avoid watching the same traffic signal change three times before it's finally your turn to go.

Combine errands into a single trip.

If you have multiple stops to make, try to combine them into just a single trip. That way, your car will have to warm up only once, and it will get the best possible fuel economy along the way. According to the U.S. Department of Energy, several short trips involving cold starts can use twice as much fuel as a single multistop trip that allows the engine to become and stay warm.

Plan your route in advance.

If you have multiple places to go during a local trip, draw either an actual or a mental map and think about the most efficient way to reach all of them. You don't need a computer and simulation software—just put some advance thought into the various possibilities and how efficient each order might tend to be. If you have a GPS navigational system, you may be able to optimize by programming your stops as "way-points" during your mission.

Make the most distant errand your first stop.

If possible, try to arrange the order of your stops so that the most distant stop is the first one you make. That way, your engine will warm up more quickly and completely, making it more efficient during subsequent legs of the trip.

Avoid back-tracking.

If possible, avoid retracing a route you've already traveled in the same direction. This will help reduce the distance you travel and the amount of gasoline you use along the way.

Check gas prices en route.

If you will be returning home along the same route, check the gas prices at stations along the way so that you can fill up with the cheapest fuel on the way back.

Choose the warmed-up vehicle.

For a local errand, take the car that's already warm. On short trips, even a warm SUV might get better mileage than a cold midsize sedan. If a member of your household has just returned from somewhere in the family SUV, it could be more efficient to take the SUV on your two-mile trip than the midsize sedan that would normally deliver 25 percent more miles per gallon. The cold engine of the sedan might achieve only half the fuel economy that it would when warm.

Take the most efficient vehicle for the job.

You don't need a sledge hammer to swat a fly. If you're on your way to Home Depot to buy a new lawn mower, take the most efficient vehicle with the space to do the job. For example, if you have two SUVs, and both are cold, take whichever one is smaller and more efficient.

Reduce the size of your fleet.

Although it's nice to be able to choose from a number of vehicles, it's possible to have too many of them. Cars like to be driven, and when they spend most of their time parked, especially outside, they will deteriorate. Those shiny brake rotors will develop surface corrosion. Sunlight and ozone will age those thick-treaded tires, and the rubber camshaft belt will begin to take on the odd shape of the circuitous route it travels along the pulleys it serves. Multiply your number of cars by four, and that's the number of tires you'll need to check each week or so, especially if some of them tend to lose a little air from one check to the next. The more cars you have, the more maintenance you'll have to perform—and if maintenance begins to slip, so will fuel economy. If your driveway is starting to look like a used car lot, consider either opening up a used car lot or saving some grief and gas money by selling the ones that are larger than what you really need.

Adjust, then start.

If you need to move the seat, adjust the mirrors, plug in your cell phone, program the GPS navigational system, and tend to various other matters, it's best to do so prior to starting the engine. That way, you can drive off as soon as the car has started, saving yourself some idling time and allowing the engine to warm up more quickly because the car will actually be moving.

Remove snow and ice.

Before you use a car that's been parked outside in a cold climate, remove any snow or ice that has accumulated. You don't have to remove absolutely all of it, but pay extra attention to the windshield and the rear window. A pile of snow on your car will make it both heavier and less aerodynamic, and a thick layer of ice left on the rear window will require you to use the energy-hungry rear window defroster for a longer time. For peak efficiency, take care of all these things before you actually start the car.

Lift and save frozen wipers.

If your car has been parked overnight in cold weather, the wipers could be frozen to the windshield, even if the glass looks relatively clear. Lift each wiper blade and flex it slightly to rid it of ice and stiffness. If you turn on the wipers when they are frozen, you can damage the wipers and their motor. And if you can't see where you're going, you can't drive very efficiently.

Get an early start.

Wherever you're going, be sure to get an on-time, if not early, start. Reading that extra section of the morning paper could lead to your having to drive quickly and inefficiently in order to get to work or school on time.

Telecommute one day a week.

If possible, work from home and communicate by phone and computer one day a week. If you can do this, you'll cut your fuel bill for commuting by 20 percent.

Shift your work hours.

Try to shift your work schedule so you still put in the same amount of time at work but spend much less time—and gas—battling traffic during your commute. Make a request to arrive late and leave late, to arrive early and leave early, or even to arrive early and leave late. The latter possibility would be difficult for any boss to turn down, but you might want to avoid asking for this particular combination.

Form or join a carpool.

By sharing the driving, you can save gas by having to drive your car to work as little as one day per week. You'll also reduce the overall number of cars on the road and emissions into the atmosphere. The downside is you may have to leave earlier, get home later, and drive around picking up your fellow carpoolers. As with errands, try to select the most efficient order in which to do the pickups.

Opt for the online course.

If you're enrolling to take those last few courses you need to graduate from your university that's fifty miles from home, save gas by signing up for the online sections if they are available.

Get a transponder for tolls.

If you frequently use toll roads, get an electronic transponder, like E-Z Pass or FasTrak, then breeze through the toll area with less braking and maximum fuel efficiency.

Exact cash at the booth.

If you must pay cash at toll booths, try to have the exact amount handy before you arrive. You won't be able to continue without stopping, but at least you'll minimize the fuel spent idling while the state collects its money.

Remove the junk from the trunk.

Most of us can make our cars lighter and more fuel efficient by simply cleaning out the trunk. You don't need to haul that anvil or chain saw back there unless you're on your way to do some blacksmithing or chain-sawing, and you surely don't need those golf clubs all the time just in case you're randomly pulled over and ordered to play eighteen holes. If you don't need it right now and it's back there, take it out. The only exceptions: tools, spare tire, and the most basic of emergency equipment. While you're at it, look through the car and remove anything else that doesn't absolutely have to be there. Excess weight is like an additional sales tax at the pump: every 100 pounds you're lugging around can reduce gas mileage as much as 2 percent. Besides clearing out the trunk, check the glove compartment, center console, the cup holders, and anywhere else where things tend to get squirreled away in your car. One researcher, in doing a bumper-to-bumper examination of the contents of a sample of cars, found cup holders in which the owner had even stashed three spools of dental floss.

Spare tires: one's enough.

One spare tire should be plenty, and it should be a compact tire for less weight. Unless you're a real weight-reduction fanatic, don't go to the extreme of filling it with helium instead of air.

Lighten up the tool collection.

Choose multipurpose tools and get an inexpensive kit with a variety of common tools in a plastic case. Carry loose tools in a cardboard box instead of a metal toolbox. Don't forget a few plastic tie wraps and a thin roll of duct tape—they're light and can fix just about anything.

Lighten up the driver and passengers.

According to the U.S. Centers for Disease Control and Prevention, two-thirds of Americans are either overweight or obese, and the average American is 23 pounds overweight. According to CDC Director Thomas Frieden, we as a nation are carrying around a total of 4.6 billion extra pounds. That spare tire you're carrying around may actually be the equivalent of an extra spare tire that your car has to carry around. Let's look at this from a more national perspective: If the average American is 23 pounds overweight, if we have 250 million U.S. adults, and the average U.S. adult travels 12,000 miles per year by car, a little math converts that into a total of 28.75 billion ton-miles, more than twice the approximately 12 billion ton-miles of all U.S. domestic air freight shipments in the most recent year reported.

What? Remove the Seats?

If your van or SUV has removable seats, you probably already know how heavy they are. If you only rarely use them, save weight and gas by removing them. If your wagon has a rear-facing third seat you haven't used since the kids grew up, take it out too. For the latter, there could be some wrenches involved, but don't remove anything if you'll need a hacksaw or torch.

Don't stop with the seats.

Consider removing other nonessential components weighing down your car, such as underhood soundproofing materials and trunk carpeting. And your neighbors probably wouldn't mind a bit if you removed that subwoofer with its heavy magnet. Alternatively, if you were to find just the right place to park your car overnight, you might arrive the next day to find that somebody else had done all the weight-loss work for you.

It takes gas to haul gas.

Gasoline weighs about 6 pounds per gallon, so if you're comfortable with a tank that's 5 gallons low most of the time, you'll improve your fuel economy by dropping another 30 pounds. It's not a good idea to carry this strategy too far, since tanks containing less fuel will contain more air, and overnight parking outside can lead to greater moisture condensation within the tank. That can lead to other kinds of problems, none of which will help your fuel economy.

Don't carry gas in the trunk.

When on a long trip, it's good to have a long driving range between fuel stops, but don't expand your car's range by carrying extra gasoline in the trunk or anywhere else on or within your vehicle. It's dangerous and it's extra weight you don't really need.

Don't drive around looking for cheap gas.

Know ahead of time where to find the cheapest gas in your area. If you're traveling, especially on the interstate, take note of gas prices posted on billboards. Don't just drive around looking for cheap gas in an unfamiliar area. Even if you happen to find an ultra-cheap place, chances are you'll have spent more money finding it than you'll save once you're there. Use a site like *www.gasbuddy.com* to get a heads-up on where to find bargain gas in your town or in places through which you'll be traveling on a trip.

Multitasking at the convenience store.

If you really need to go to the local convenience store for that two-liter bottle of diet whatever, and you could also use some gas, park at the pump, fill up, then leave the car there while you go inside to get the items you came for. You can pay for everything at once, and you'll minimize the damage to your fuel economy by only restarting the car once. This works best when the pump lanes aren't crowded and nobody's getting impatient out there.

Shop locally.

By shopping near your home, you'll not only save gas, you will be helping your local economy as well.

Shop big.

Purchase items in larger quantities. This will reduce the number of shopping trips you'll have to make, and you'll be saving gasoline in the process.

Shop where you can fulfill many needs.

Instead of driving to different stores for different things, save gas by shopping where you can obtain most of the goods and services you need at the same place. Besides the convenience and fuel savings, the prices will likely be lower as well.

Park as soon as you can.

No matter how hard it's raining, don't spend five minutes driving around the mall parking lot looking for the one space that's the absolute closest to the entrance you'll be using. Just park and walk. Burning calories and saving gas are both good ideas.

Shop online or by telephone.

You'll save miles and gas, and you won't have to worry about your car getting bumped by a wayward shopping cart.

Comparison shop online beforehand.

Regardless of what you're buying, you can find out specifications, relative prices, owner comments and satisfaction ratings, and a great deal more by doing some research on the Internet before you go to the store. Besides becoming a more knowledgeable shopper, you'll save yourself a lot of time, driving, and gas.

Take mini-vacations.

Instead of taking one long vacation during which you drive and tour, then arrive home exhausted, be more refreshed and save gas by taking several mini-vacations during the year at a variety of attractive areas that are much closer to home.

Alternatives to a driving vacation.

Instead of taking a driving vacation that uses a lot of gasoline, stay home and spend the vacation and gas money on something you can enjoy during all fifty-two weeks of the year, like a large flat-screen, wall-mounted television. Be sure to watch the Travel Channel. If you're not into TV, just get out and do something different in your own hometown, maybe visit the local historical society, get some extra exercise, or volunteer at a local nonprofit organization or animal shelter.

Vacation in the off-season.

Schedule your vacation for the off-season. You'll enjoy cheaper gasoline, fewer crowds, less traffic, and cheaper room rates—overall, a nice combination.

Don't rule out a camping vacation.

If, despite high fuel prices, you're considering buying or renting a camping trailer for your vacation, don't despair. The so-called "pop-up" campers are aerodynamic and have a low profile on the road but can be cranked upward and outward to become quite roomy at the campground. They "draft" closely behind your vehicle for low aerodynamic drag and, at highway cruising speeds, don't use much more fuel than if you had simply piled a lot of stuff on the roof of your car. In on-road tests, a compact car pulling a 1,310-pound, 7-sleeper, pop-up camper at a steady 55 miles per hour required only 1.29 more gallons of gas per 100 miles compared to an extra 0.96 gallons per 100 miles required by a rooftop carrier with a total weight of just 120 pounds.

Get a room. In advance.

If you're staying overnight at least once during a trip, plan your route and make reservations ahead of time. You won't have to waste gas by driving around looking for vacancies in an unfamiliar area. If you have a GPS navigational system, you can enjoy the added flexibility of locating and reserving an alternative room en route. This can be useful because you'll have a better idea of how far you'll feel like traveling on a given day. If you overbook, don't forget to call and cancel before the deadline.

Prepare a "cheat sheet" for rarely taken routes.

If you don't have a GPS navigational system, put together a cheat sheet for trips that you only occasionally make, such as to the home of a distant friend or relative. This should include key odometer readings, exit numbers, notes on which lanes to use in congested areas, and even the locations of gas stations or restaurants to be frequented or avoided. This is old-fashioned compared to today's sophisticated navigational systems, but it works, and it will help you avoid wasting fuel as you wander around trying to remember where that turn is you made two years ago.

Contingency routes.

Regardless of the length of your trip, you're bound to run into delays caused by highway construction and accidents. Before you leave home, figure out a few alternate routes that will help you avoid sitting in fuel-wasting traffic.

Traveling: set your GPS navigational system to "maximize freeway."

If you have a GPS navigational system, you can save gas on a long trip by setting it to maximize interstate or freeway travel. Freeway travel may sometimes be longer than invoking the shortcuts taken by long-time locals, but you'll maintain momentum, use the brakes less often, and get better fuel economy along the way.

Traveling: avoid or deal with rush hour in waypoint cities.

If you take the beltway around a major city, you'll be traveling more miles compared to simply taking the interstate straight through the center of the city. But the beltway alternative might be better if you happen to arrive at a metropolitan area during rush hour. If you've set your GPS navigational system to maximize freeway use, it might stubbornly persist in having you join the other 20,000 poor souls creeping through the center of the city during rush hour. In this case, you should stubbornly resist, and save fuel by taking the beltway instead.

The "see" rule.

Before you leave the interstate for the food or fuel you've seen advertised on a billboard, consider the "see" rule: If you can't see the establishment or its sign from the interstate, keep on going. Don't get caught chasing a restaurant that is five or six miles from the interstate. Falling for this ruse wastes both time and fuel. Also, it's usually best to pull off for food or gasoline only at exits where you know there are at least two or three businesses of each type advertised prior to the exit.

No hitchhikers.

Regardless of how much you want to help, do not pick up hitch-hikers during your journey. Besides adding weight and creating an extra stop or two, they will distract you from your task of driving efficiently and might even be dangerous.

Driveway maneuvering.

Try to avoid having to back out of your driveway, especially if you live on a busy street or highway. Also, back-and-forth maneuvering is more efficient when the engine is warm, so each time you return from a trip, save gas by preparing for a frontward exit for your next trip.

Garage your car between trips.

During colder weather, this will help fuel efficiency by making sure the car is a little warmer when you start it, thus reducing the time it takes to reach efficient operating temperature. It will also improve the life of rubber and plastic components that are susceptible to deterioration when exposed to sunlight, heat, and other elements.

Convert your garage into a garage.

For many, the garage eventually becomes a crowded storage place where there is no room for the car it's supposed to accommodate. For the sake of your car and fuel efficiency, use your garage to store cars, not junk.

Use the warmest part of the garage.

Especially during cold weather, park your car so the front of the car is as close as possible to the warmest portion of the garage. This improves fuel efficiency by allowing the engine to warm up more quickly the next time you start it up.

Un-trash your car.

In a household with multiple drivers and multiple vehicles, the most efficient car should be used as often as possible. However, if the most efficient vehicle is cluttered with McDonald's bags, candy wrappers, soda cans, and other trash, nobody is going to want to drive it. Household trash isn't very heavy, so it doesn't have much direct effect on fuel economy. But if you clean up your car so it looks like a car instead of a garbage dumpster, other members of your household will be more likely to save fuel by actually driving it.

Pushing to wash or mow.

If your garage and driveway are level, and you need to move the car briefly from the garage to wash it or to access the riding mower, it's a waste of gas to start the car and drive it 20 feet or so. If possible, release the brake, put the transmission in neutral, and very slowly and carefully push the car out of the garage. Have somebody sit in the driver's seat, ready to apply the parking brake if needed. When you're ready to put it back, save another cold start by pushing it back in. Also, if the garage and driveway are level and you are unable to move the car by pushing it, you may have more problems than a car that needs washed or grass that needs cut—your brakes may be dragging and in need of inspection or repair.

Garage floor cardboard.

Placing a bit of cardboard on the garage floor beneath the engine will help you detect fluid leaks that could indicate problems adversely affecting your fuel economy. Most cars over a few years old will tend to drip at least a little bit of something or other, but if you see more than a couple of drops, something is amiss. Different fluids will tend to have different colors—e.g., automatic transmission fluid tends to be red and coolant may be green or orange. Besides helping you head off problems before they get serious, the cardboard will also help keep the garage floor clean.

Street parking.

In urban areas, you may need to park on the street and expose your bumpers to other street-parkers. Front ends, front bumpers, and front air deflectors aren't as aerodynamic when they've been battered, so try to protect the front more than the rear. When possible, park at the front of the block or have your front end exactly on the legal side of the "no parking" yellow line. The front end is not only more expensive to repair, it's also the more important end when it comes to aerodynamics and fuel efficiency.

Use a windshield sun reflector.

When parking on hot days, use an aluminized sun reflector that fits into the windshield area and helps prevent excess heat from building up inside the car. A super-hot interior will cause you to use more gasoline trying to cool things down. Be sure the "Send Help" side of the reflector is not facing outward.

Cold? Park sunny and bright.

On cold days, park in a sunny or bright location that will help keep the engine compartment and interior as warm as possible. This will help the engine to warm up and reach its efficient operating temperature more quickly.

Monitor your car's fuel consumption.

In industry, there's a saying that goes, "If you want to improve it, you have to be able to measure it." The same is true of fuel economy. Monitoring and measuring fuel consumption as you take steps to improve it will help you see what really works and inspire you to get even better.

The break-in effect.

If you've just purchased a new car, your fuel efficiency might be a little disappointing at first. But don't worry; brand-new machinery requires at least a little break-in time during which mechanical components and their frictional neighbors get to know each other a little better and smooth out little imperfections. This usually takes somewhere between 3,000 and 5,000 miles. Be sure to follow the manufacturer's recommendations for driving strategies or speed during those first few thousand miles. Whatever you do, absolutely do not delay the initial oil change and the maintenance procedures that go with it.

Keep cumulative records.

Don't just record mileage and fuel consumption for your most recent road trip. It may have been from a high-altitude city to a low-altitude city, or assisted by the prevailing winds that tend to go from west to east. Even if you just compare fuel economy data from one month to the next, that's better than getting trapped in the small tank-to-tank picture that provides little information on the improvements you're achieving.

Help family and friends.

Nothing gets on people's nerves more than somebody critiquing their driving. Encourage your family and friends to drive efficiently, but be aware that your observations or nagging could end up having an effect directly opposite the one you wish to achieve. Either loan them this book, or (preferably) give them a copy as a gift. Nobody likes a back-seat driver.

CHAPTER 4

Buying a New Vehicle

Be immune to showroom fever.

Buy an efficient automobile that best suits your typical needs, not the larger vehicle you might need just once or twice a year. Soccer coaches and electricians might really need a lot of hauling capacity, but do you? If you only rarely need the greater capacity of a truck, van, or SUV, rent one with some of the gas money you save the rest of the year. Better yet, don't we all have a friend, neighbor, or relative with a pickup truck? Don't be hypnotized by showroom glitter and fast talk, and don't allow yourself to be rushed. If it's really the right vehicle for you, it will still be the right vehicle after you've left the showroom and had a good night's sleep.

Buy a full hybrid vehicle.

A full hybrid has a gasoline engine that provides most of its power, plus a relatively large electric motor for additional power as needed.

The electric motor is even large enough to power the car and accessories all by itself at low speeds. Energy for the electric motor is stored in a large battery pack that is charged in two ways. The first is regenerative braking, a process by which the electric motor becomes a generator when the brakes are applied, slowing the car while sending electricity to the batteries. The second is through normal operation of the gasoline engine, especially during downhill and coasting conditions. Regenerative braking is a great concept: Much of the heat and friction that would ordinarily result from braking in a conventional vehicle is being transformed into electrical energy and stored for future use. Besides your fuel lasting much longer, your brake life should drastically increase as well. The best-known full hybrid is the Toyota Prius, with estimated EPA ratings of 51 mpg (city) and 48 mpg (highway) for the 2011 model. This is the third generation of this vehicle, and future models will undoubtedly do even better. According to IntelliChoice.com, an automotive industry research site, the sticker price of the Toyota Prius is about $2,000 higher than that of the comparable entry-level Toyota Camry, but will save its owner nearly $5,000 over five years of ownership—not a bad investment, eh?

Consider other hybrids as well.

If a full hybrid doesn't suit your needs, there are other variations available. As with the full hybrid, these have a gasoline engine and an electric motor that provides additional power and gets its energy from a battery pack and regenerative braking. However, in these models, the electric motor is smaller and isn't used to power the vehicle and accessories on its own. Nevertheless, you still get the considerable advantage of regenerative braking that converts much of the braking energy that would otherwise be wasted and turns it into electricity for future use. In some of these vehicles, both the gasoline engine and the electric motor are small. In others, the gasoline engine is quite powerful on its own, and the hybrid concept is being used more for the purpose of improving fuel economy while enhancing the performance of what is already a very high-performing vehicle.

Get in line for a plug-in hybrid.

Owning a plug-in hybrid is like having a gas station in your garage, but you'll be pumping electricity instead of gasoline. As it sits in your garage, your hybrid's battery pack will become fully charged from a normal wall socket and extension cord, and your car will use this electricity to help you save even more gasoline on your next trip. In the very near future, there will be an impressive number of plug-in hybrids available, but you still have a chance to be near the head of the line.

An electric car, perhaps?

For local trips and short commutes, an electric vehicle might be a good addition to your garage. Some of these models will have no gasoline engine at all, and the car will run entirely on electricity from its battery pack, with the electricity coming from a garage wall socket via your friendly local power company. One such car already on the road is the Tesla Roadster, which has only an electric motor—but it's a big one. Imagine 0–60 mph acceleration in 3.9 seconds, a top speed of 125 mph, and a 245-mile driving range on a single charge. For most of us, imagination is as far as we'll get, for the price of admission to this high-performance machine is in the neighborhood of $100,000. A more affordable and primarily electric car for the rest of us is the Chevy Volt, introduced in the 2011 model year. Its engineers creatively combined a small gasoline engine with an electric motor to form what ends up being an efficient and effective marriage. As with a pure electric car, the battery pack is charged from the wall socket and the car will traverse a typical commuter round-trip distance on electricity alone. The small gasoline engine is not directly connected to the wheels, it never actually drives the car in the conventional sense, and the only time it runs is when the batteries run down and need charging. The Volt can go about 35 miles on a single charge. If the batteries run down, the gasoline engine/generator kicks in and allows up to 340 extra miles. Try not to use the 100 mph top speed.

If you really need a pickup or SUV.

If you really need a pickup or SUV, do the best you can. Choose a hybrid or diesel version if available, and don't buy anything larger or more fuel-inefficient than you absolutely must. Consider crossover vehicles, which are a mix of car and SUV, since one of these might suit your purposes just fine.

How about a diesel?

Diesel engines have no spark plugs and ignite the air-fuel mixture simply by generating very high pressure within the cylinders. In the 1980s and 1990s, they got a bad reputation for being slow and putting out a lot of noise and soot. However, newer models tend to be turbocharged, run on ultra-low-sulfur fuel, and make use of advanced engine and exhaust technologies to deliver good performance and about 30–35 percent more mpg than a gasoline engine of comparable size. One of the reasons is that diesel fuel contains about 10 percent more energy per gallon than gasoline.

The diesel version might cost a little more to buy, but consider it an investment with an excellent rate of return. According to a study by automotive industry website IntelliChoice.com, the Volkswagen Jetta TDI Clean Diesel costs about $2,000 more than its gasoline-powered counterpart. However, over a five-year period, the combination of higher resale value, along with lower maintenance and fuel costs, saves the owner $6,200. Even Ponzi investment schemes like the one operated by the convicted Bernie Madoff would be hard-pressed to promise such a high rate of return, but the diesel investment is one you can actually count on. Those who like to continue driving "until I get there" may appreciate yet another benefit: Because the diesel version of a vehicle typically has the same size fuel tank as its gasoline counterpart, the driving range on a tank will astound both you and your passengers, and chances are the limiting factor between stops will be your own physical needs and endurance.

Flex-fuel vehicles.

Although not yet in the mainstream, efficient vehicles running on alternative fuels are available and increasing in popularity. Typical flex-fuel vehicles have just one fuel tank, fuel system, and engine, but are designed to run on gasoline, E85 (a blend with 15 percent gasoline and 85 percent ethanol), or any mixture in between. Ethanol is made from corn and other crops, and unlike fossil fuels, it has the advantage of being a renewable resource. However, your fuel economy with E85 will be 25–30 percent lower because a gallon of ethanol contains less energy than a gallon of gasoline. When you're buying fuel, you might want to think of ethanol as diluted gasoline, so be sure to do your math when you're comparing the prices at the pump.

Look into other alternative-fuel vehicles.

Currently, other alternative-fuel vehicles to consider may be powered by biodiesel (derived from vegetable oils and animal fats), CNG (compressed natural gas), or LPG (liquefied petroleum gas). Although they are still in development and not yet ready for the mass market, there are also fuel-cell vehicles that use hydrogen as a fuel. These are typically powered by electric motors driven by the energy produced when oxygen combines with the hydrogen gas stored onboard in high-pressure tanks. The end result is an exhaust that is nothing more than harmless water vapor.

Consider a motorcycle or scooter.

If you're used to four-wheel travel and $50 fill-ups, you'll be amazed at the amount of fuel you'll save by riding a motorcycle or scooter. They're inexpensive to buy and operate, parking is easy, and they're fun when the weather is good. Just be sure to drive very defensively, since you'll likely be surrounded by vehicles many times your size and mass, and at least one of their drivers may be distracted as they're putting in a new CD, texting, or receiving a cell phone call.

Your next car: a bike!

With a bicycle, you can travel a lot of miles using zero gallons of gas, but weather and traffic could be problematic. Nevertheless, your health and budget could both benefit if a bike path happens to connect where you live with where you work. A lot of people are already commuting by bike: A 2007 American Community Survey by the U.S. Census Bureau showed that 0.48 percent of workers, or about 650,000 people, were using their bikes to get to and from work, and the percentage is increasing every year.

Buy a complementing car.

On a football team, we have players of different sizes and skill sets playing different positions, and the team works a lot better this way. Do you really need two subcompacts or two SUVs? With two different kinds of vehicles available, you can choose the one that fits your need for any given trip or job. Caution: Before buying, be sure to have some operational agreement as to how you're going to go about sharing.

Look for a small frontal area.

With other factors about equal, look for a vehicle with a smaller frontal area—this is a function of the height and width of the vehicle. Vehicles with a smaller frontal area will tend to make a smaller "hole" in the air through which they are traveling, and this means less wind resistance and less fuel consumed.

Go streamlined, and not just from the front.

In wind tunnel tests, the drag coefficient is one indication of how much wind resistance a vehicle is likely to encounter, based on its shape, as it travels through the air. Look for the drag coefficient (Cd) in the vehicle specifications, and remember that lower is better. Note that when you drive through a crosswind, your car is essentially moving slightly sideways relative to the air around it. Because some cars are more efficient than others under these conditions, try to visualize how aerodynamic your car might be if it were going slightly sideways instead of forward.

Ground clearance: lower is better.

"Clearance" is good when we're referring to sales at Sears, but not so good when we are trying to get more miles per gallon. At highway speeds, greater ground clearance provides more space and opportunity for the aerodynamic drag caused by air turbulence beneath your vehicle. On the other hand, gasoline is cheaper than replacing exhaust systems, engine crankcases, and transmission housings, so if your travels often take you off-road, go for the clearance.

Buy light: weight costs fuel.

As Sir Isaac Newton once noted, objects at rest tend to stay at rest and objects in motion tend to stay in motion. Had Sir Isaac owned an automobile, he would have noticed that heavier cars need more gasoline to get moving, and more energy to bring them to a stop. Heavier vehicles also encounter greater rolling resistance, which also eats up fuel. With all else being relatively equal, a vehicle that is 500 pounds heavier will get approximately 2 to 5 fewer miles per gallon.

Opt for the base engine.

If you prefer a conventional gasoline engine, choose the standard version. Many models have a four-cylinder "base" engine, with an optional V6. If this is the case, go for the four and enjoy a few more miles per gallon. The V6-capable engine compartment will be roomy, so service may be cheaper and easier for you or your mechanic to perform. If you're a do-it-yourselfer, the extra space in the engine compartment will also help you save money on bandages and tetanus shots, and your kids won't learn as many bad words when they're watching you work on the car.

Look for engine technology features.

Many of today's vehicles have one or more of the following energy-efficient engine technologies (note fuel efficiency gain in parentheses):

- Variable valve timing and lift: optimizes flow of fuel and air into the cylinders (5 percent).
- Cylinder deactivation: shuts down some of the cylinders when they aren't needed (7.5 percent).
- Turbochargers and superchargers: increases power from smaller engines (7.5 percent).
- Integrated starter/generator (ISG): automatically turns engine off when vehicle is stopped (8 percent).
- Direct fuel injection: injects fuel directly into the cylinders and is used with turbocharger or supercharger (12 percent).

Continuously variable transmission.

One of the major transmission technologies currently available is the continuously variable transmission (CVT). It uses a belt or chain to transmit power from one variable-diameter pulley to another. This is the equivalent of having an infinite number of "gears," and it allows the engine to run steadily at its most efficient speed, gaining an estimated 6 percent in fuel efficiency. At least initially, it can be a little disconcerting when the engine speed stays the same regardless of how fast the car is moving.

Automated manual transmission.

Automated manual transmission (AMT) combines the convenience of an automatic with the efficiency of a manual. There is no clutch, shifting can be done manually or controlled electronically, and the estimated gain in fuel efficiency is 7 percent.

Electrically powered engine cooling fan.

Many of today's cars don't have a fan belt because their engine cooling fans are activated only when the engine needs them, such as when driving at low speeds or poking along in city traffic. This type of fan is powered by electricity and controlled by a sensor that monitors the coolant temperature. At highway speeds, lots of air is being pushed through the radiator, so there's no need for a cooling fan and the energy it consumes.

The right kind of running lights.

"Lights on for safety" is a nice slogan, and having your headlights on in the daytime can make your car more noticeable and you more safe. However, lights use electricity and electricity uses fuel, so you may prefer a vehicle in which you can turn off the daytime running lights if you wish. However, some vehicle manufacturers give you no choice in the matter. If this is the case, always remember to turn on your "real" lights (which include the very-important tail lights) as darkness approaches.

Do you need air conditioning?

If A/C is not standard equipment on the vehicle you are considering, keep in mind that air conditioning uses energy, and that energy comes from the fuel we buy. According to the Environmental Protection Agency, operating the air conditioning at its maximum output can reduce fuel economy by anywhere from 5 to 25 percent compared to identical situations in which the air conditioning is not used. Even when not in use, A/C reduces fuel economy simply because of the extra weight of its compressor and other components. On the other hand, there are some locales where you can barely exist without air conditioning, let alone drive without it. The bottom line: It's your comfort, your money, and your choice.

Opt out of the electric seat warmer.

They may be comfy, but these things use a lot of electricity, and—once again—using electricity requires you to burn gasoline. Either wear warmer clothing or be patient until you warm up the seat the old-fashioned way: by sitting on it.

Consider a manual transmission.

If a lot of your driving is on the highway, consider the 5- or 6-speed manual transmission. Compared to the conventional automatic transmission, manual transmissions absorb less power, weigh less, tend to get more miles per gallon, are cheaper to buy, and cost way less to repair. Unfortunately, both manual transmissions and the number of people who know how to drive them are on the decline. According to consultancy firm AutoPacific, only about 5 percent of U.S. auto buyers opt for a manual transmission when they buy a new car. This is partly explained by the fact that many manufacturers offer the stick shift only in their ultra-high-performance cars or in their cheapest and least desirable models—and neither end of the spectrum has many top-sellers. Yet another explanation comes from marital/partnership relationships and associated skill sets. If you can drive a manual and your partner can only drive an automatic, take just one guess as to which type of transmission will be in your next new car? If you want to persist, and without chipping the gears in your own ride, consider a short-term rental vehicle for teaching your spouse/partner the basics of clutch, brake, gas pedal, and shift lever coordination. For the beginner, these are a lot of things to keep in mind at the same time, so make sure he or she is not chewing gum or jiving to the radio during your lessons.

With automatics, opt for overdrive.

In general, a 6-speed automatic transmission will have a more long-legged (fewer engine revolutions per mile) overdrive top gear than its 5-speed counterpart. Likewise, a 5-speed will tend to have a more relaxing top gear than its 4-speed counterpart. Automatics with a top-gear overdrive feature may also have a "lock-out" button on or near the transmission lever that prevents the overdrive from engaging. Use of this switch will reduce your annoyance when you're climbing a hill and your transmission keeps changing its mind as to whether it wants the top gear or the next one down.

With automatic transmission, be sure it "locks-up" in top gear.

A conventional automatic transmission has a torque converter that slips a little in the lower gears. This makes the gear changes smoother, but it also reduces the efficiency with which power is transmitted from the engine to the wheels. As you're cruising along at a steady 30 mph, you'll notice that your tachometer needle drops rapidly when you take your foot off the gas and rises rapidly when you press harder on the gas. When the lock-up feature activates in top gear, changes in vehicle speed and changes in engine speed will coincide because the torque converter has locked up, eliminating the slippage that occurs in the lower gears. The lock-up is a great feature, especially at highway speeds when it can make your car as efficient as one with a manual transmission.

Under-hood indicators: where's the oil filter?

Look under the hood. Can you see the spark plugs? The oil filter? Anything other than a jumble of wires and hoses and a neat-looking engine cover? If not, and if you're the kind of person who wants to save money and enhance fuel efficiency by changing your own oil, keep in mind that a lot of today's engines don't make it easy. If you're a dedicated do-it-yourselfer, you may find that some seemingly simple procedures require expensive special tools or are overly complex. If this might cause you to put off or neglect to do routine maintenance, keep shopping.

How complete is the owner's manual?

Does the manufacturer include advice on efficient driving for that model; starting advice for hot, cold, and frigid conditions; and technical information such as the electrical system fuse locations and the number of foot-pounds of torque to which the wheel bolts or lug nuts should be tightened? Some manuals simply present descriptions and explanations for instruments and controls, and "see dealer" is the universal response for many situations you or your mechanically inclined nephew could have handled on your own. Ask to see the manual before you buy, because this information is important and could save you gas and a whole lot more.

When and where was the car made?

Information regarding the location and date of manufacture is generally located on a sticker on the driver's door or its frame. This can be important to note, as the manufacturer may have made small improvements during the year that could affect the fuel efficiency and general operating capabilities of the vehicle. Furthermore, batteries and rubber components gradually deteriorate from age or exposure to sunlight, and newer is better. When you go to the grocery store, you don't search out the milk container with the oldest "best if purchased by" date, do you? You deserve no less when buying your car. Finally, some manufacturing plants may have better reputations than others when it comes to fit-and-finish and other aspects of product quality, and this sticker can let you know where your car was born.

Opt for the pull-up parking brake.

The pull-up parking or emergency brake is preferable to the step-on version for a couple of reasons: First, you can press the release button and easily control the position of the lever and the braking force it exerts, making the device actually useful for emergency stops. Second, if you have a manual transmission, the pull-up brake makes it easier for you to start from an uphill stop, thus saving the fuel loss and clutch wear that would otherwise result from your drifting backward while you're moving your right foot from the brake pedal to the accelerator pedal.

Brakes: discs versus drums.

Disc brakes have many engineering advantages, and most high-quality cars are equipped with discs all around. However, they can drag when the pads do not fully retract from the disc (or rotor) that they have just pinched in order to stop or slow the car. This drag is usually minimal, but it will still waste a bit of gasoline. On the other hand, a properly adjusted drum brake should have no drag at all, but a possible glitch here can be the self-adjuster mechanism that automatically tightens up the brake adjustment to compensate for lining wear. Sometimes this well-meaning feature can be a little too ambitious, thinking you'll be happy if your drum brakes drag just a little. Know what you're buying and understand the advantages and disadvantages that come with your brakes.

Opt for the compact spare tire.

The compact spare tire is so tiny, it doesn't even look like a real tire. However, it saves fuel by virtue of its light weight, and it also make extra room in the trunk so you can better avoid having to put things on the roof.

Read a good tire lately?

You may look at the "P195/65R15 89S" on one of the tires of your potential new car and be instantly confused. Here's the translation: P = passenger tire, 195 = tire width (in millimeters), 65 = aspect ratio (the cross section of the tire is 65 percent as high as it is wide), R = radial ply construction, 15 = diameter (in inches) of the wheel on which the tire is mounted, 89 = load rating index for the tire, and S = speed rating. The U.S. Department of Transportation also requires that tires be labeled with regard to tread wear rating, traction, and temperature resistance. Tires with radial-ply construction will have lower rolling resistance than their bias-ply counterparts, and these are the tires most likely to be found on new cars today. Tires with a high tread wear index will generally be of high quality and have relatively low rolling resistance. For best fuel efficiency, opt for a car with radial tires having a higher aspect ratio (i.e., "skinnier") and a high tread wear index.

Avoid ultra-low-profile tire options.

Be wary of option packages that include ultra-low-profile tires. These are tires with an extremely low aspect ratio, meaning their cross section will be very low and very wide. The handling and cornering will be amazing, and the tires will look very impressive. However, their costly wheels will be more susceptible to pothole damage, the tires themselves will be expensive to replace, and you can expect both greater rolling resistance and higher fuel consumption.

Alloy wheels are lighter.

Naturally, alloy wheels cost a little more, but they are lighter and more fuel efficient than their steel counterparts. If possible, opt for the alloy wheels, but try to avoid the wider tires that often accompany them.

Steel wheels and their fragile covers.

To avoid having your friends think you were cheap, manufacturers thoughtfully provide plastic wheel covers that (at least from a distance) make it look like you bought alloy wheels instead of steel. These covers are often held in place in flimsy fashion, they are large in diameter, and their fastening components can be easily snapped or broken if you don't happen to use the perfect technique in removing or replacing them. When you have your wheels spun-balanced, as you should, the proper weights are applied in accordance to what the wheel and tire assembly requires, and the wheel cover is not included in that operation. Thus, when you then reinstall a broken or badly centered wheel cover you will have disrupted your mechanic's good intentions and may end up with a wheel that is just as out of balance as before. Out-of-balance wheels are not only annoying and hard on suspension components, they lead to flat spots and other problems with your tires, and tires roll more easily and require less fuel when they are round.

The "low tire pressure" warning device.

Tire pressure monitoring systems might be offered as part of an option package on some larger vehicles, but they have been mandated by federal law on all cars and light-duty vehicles since 2007. The devices can be useful in identifying sudden leaks or punctures, but don't use this system as a substitute for the good sense of occasionally checking that your tires have proper pressure for safety and low rolling resistance. Tire pressure monitoring systems can be either indirect or direct in their operation. The indirect method keeps track of how fast the four wheels are rotating and alerts you when a tire with low pressure is being forced to rotate significantly faster than the others. This kind of system may require periodic recalibration, and it might be fooled whenever all four tires happen to be low. The direct approach is preferable, as it includes a battery-powered sensor within the tire valve or wheel interior. On the downside, those little batteries will eventually run out of electricity, and they will be a lot more expensive to replace compared to the ones powering your digital bathroom scale.

Tire valve convenience.

If you have to remove the wheel covers on your car's steel wheels to reach the tire valves, that's not a sign of good engineering. Also, mechanics don't always install the wheel covers so that the tire valve actually protrudes from the opening into which it's supposed to fit. In any case, the tire valves should be as easy to reach with a simple bicycle pump as they are with the compressor nozzle at the gas station. If you can't reach them, you can't pump them. Hint: Auto supply stores sell tire valve extensions, a product you probably wouldn't want to install permanently, but just one of these can be temporarily screwed onto each valve as you go around adjusting the tire pressures, then removed so it won't be sticking way out and making your car look like it was put together by amateurs.

Variable intermittent windshield wipers.

Most cars have an intermittent windshield wiper feature whereby the wipers take a pass every five seconds or so. This is handy when rainfall is light and you would be wasting electricity and fuel by running your wipers continuously. However, not all light rainfalls are equally light, and there will be times when you might want your wipers to pass every 10 seconds instead of every 5. Variable intermittent wipers allow you to choose the time between cycles. This saves electricity, and fuel, decreases wiper and windshield wear, and allows you to more easily spot and avoid those inevitable potholes that seem intent on altering your front-end alignment.

Cruise control.

This is a must-have feature for anyone who even occasionally drives more than two miles from home on flat roads and would like to maintain a constant speed. Cruise control makes interstate driving more relaxing, and you'll avoid those forgetful moments when your right foot gets too heavy and you find yourself driving at an unsafe or inefficient speed.

Front-wheel drive.

For most people, front-wheel drive will provide all the traction they need. Compared to rear-wheel drive, there will be less energy absorbed by driveline components and no need to augment winter traction by carrying those 100-pound sandbags in the trunk.

Traction control.

Even in a front-wheel-drive vehicle, traction control is a good idea. With this feature, front wheels do a better job of cooperating with each other to decide how best to get you moving again. Front-wheel-drive cars with traction control also offer plenty of traction and handling but consume less fuel than competitors in which all four wheels are driving all the time—even if you haven't seen any ice on the roads for the past five years.

Four-wheel or all-wheel drive.

Four-wheel drive or all-wheel drive can provide added traction and a feeling of security under slippery conditions, but the extra driveline components add weight and absorb energy, even when they are not transmitting power. According to Natural Resources Canada, the weight and friction of these extra driveline parts can increase fuel consumption by 5 to 10 percent compared with two-wheel-drive vehicles.

The advantage of a turbocharger.

The turbocharger, briefly discussed earlier, is standard equipment on many vehicles. It is positioned early in the exhaust stream and increases engine efficiency by using the heat and flow of the exhaust gases to rotate at a high speed and force-feed air into the engine. Turbocharging can improve fuel economy by about 8 percent. If you stop just after climbing a long hill or cruising at interstate speeds, manufacturers often recommend that you do not shut down the engine before letting it idle for a minute or two to allow the turbocharger bearings to cool down.

Opt for a locking gas cap.

If you're going to pay all that money for gas, take some precautions to ensure that it doesn't become somebody else's gas. This is a small item that the salesperson might not mind throwing in to close the deal. Be sure to make an extra key.

Choose lightweight carpeting and mats.

Thick, plush carpeting looks nice, adds a luxury touch, and helps protect the floor from dirt and slush, but it adds weight and reduces fuel efficiency. You won't have any choice but to accept whatever carpeting comes with your car. However, if you're going to be using rubber mats to protect the carpeting that is protecting the floor, at least opt for the lightest possible mats for the amount of carpet and floor protection you need.

Mud flaps?

These can be useful in protecting your vehicle and the ones behind you from gravel, water spray, and slush. On the negative side, they add extra weight and they can also reduce fuel economy by making your vehicle less aerodynamic.

Permanent roof bars.

This is a feature available on many wagons, crossovers, and SUVs, and they are not easy to find and install as an aftermarket item. The ability to haul things on the roof (only when absolutely necessary, of course) is a nice convenience that could enable us to get by with buying a smaller vehicle instead of a larger one. The aerodynamic cost of the adjustable sideways bars is especially great—if possible, remove them for everyday driving.

Trip computer with mpg feature.

This feature serves a variety of useful purposes, not the least of which is to enable you to experiment with different speeds, routes, and driving techniques, then observe the fuel efficiency of the results. As a multiple-use device that can entertain, inform, and educate, the trip computer can help you be a more patient, moderate, and efficient driver.

GPS navigational systems.

Regardless of how great your fuel economy is, it will be to no avail if you're driving in the wrong direction or going in circles. These devices can be helpful in guiding you practically anywhere, including dining and overnight accommodations, and even how to get to the new babysitter's house. Just enter an address or telephone number, and you're efficiently on your way. The advance notice the system provides for lane changes and turns is especially comforting when you're traveling through unfamiliar areas where your fellow motorists are all in a hurry and everyone but you seems to know exactly where they are going.

The window antenna.

One of many small items that contribute to better fuel economy, an antenna that's either embedded within or mounted on the surface of the windshield can help reduce aerodynamic drag, especially at highway speeds. It also offers the side advantage of being more difficult for vandals to bend.

Read the EPA's *Fuel Economy Guide.*

Published annually by the U.S. Environmental Protection Agency (EPA), this guide provides model-specific fuel economy estimates for both city and highway travel. The data are generated under laboratory conditions but are useful in comparing the relative efficiency of the vehicles you are considering. Get a copy of the guide at practically any auto dealership or download it from their fuel efficiency website (*www.fueleconomy.gov*) before you shop.

Understand the EPA estimates.

The EPA *Fuel Economy Guide* is a handy tool for comparing city and highway mpg estimates for different vehicles, but you may find that their results, achieved in a laboratory setting, aren't precise indicators of the actual mileage your car will deliver on the road. For example, each EPA test cycle assumes that the vehicle is being driven on a paved road and according to a very strict schedule of time and speed. Four-wheel-drive vehicles are operated in two-wheel-drive mode, there are no crosswinds, and ambient temperatures are closely controlled. Beginning with the 2008 model year, tests involve more aggressive acceleration and braking, and the city and highway estimates are also lower because of downward adjustments from three new cycles—a cold-temperature variant of the city test (20 degrees Fahrenheit), a high-temperature air conditioning test (95 degrees Fahrenheit), and a high-speed test (up to 80 miles per hour). During the 31 minutes of the city test, the average speed is 21 miles per hour, the engine spends 6 minutes idling, and there are 23 stops along the way. During the 13-minute highway test, the average speed is 48 miles per hour, the top speed is 60 miles per hour, the engine is warmed up before the test begins, and there are no stops along the way.

Making best use of the EPA estimates.

From the first testing in 1985 through the 2007 model year, EPA city and highway estimates were optimistic, and drivers often complained to the dealer when their vehicle didn't live up to the laboratory numbers on the window sticker. With the test revisions in 2008, fuel economy estimates became less optimistic, more achievable, and, according to the EPA, more realistic. You may wonder if garaging your car at 20 degrees Fahrenheit, then cranking up the air conditioning when it it's 95 degrees outside constitutes realism, but that's another story. There are two morals to this tip: First, don't think you're an efficient driver just because you're exceeding the EPA estimates for your vehicle. Second, when choosing your vehicle, rely more heavily on either the city estimate or the highway estimate, depending on where you will be doing most of your driving. Finally, note that hybrids often have a strong advantage in the city, where there are many stops and regenerative braking stores electricity and saves fuel, but they are much less superior during lengthy highway trips where speeds are high and stops are few.

Opt for a sunroof.

Besides fresh air and a view of the sky, a sunroof can often provide fairly good ventilation and aerodynamics when you might otherwise be using the air conditioning or lowering all the windows. To eliminate or reduce wind buffeting, make sure yours comes with a wind deflector that pops up to reduce or eliminate turbulence when the sunroof is opened.

Avoid the vinyl roof.

A vinyl-coated roof might look nice, but it will reduce fuel economy by increasing surface friction and aerodynamic drag. Also, if you live in a very hot climate, it may fade or peel after a few years of baking in the blistering sun.

Drop the drop-top.

Everybody loves a convertible, but when the top goes down, so does your fuel economy. That wind blowing through your hair is just a small part of the turbulence that is trying to slow your car as it passes through the air. A sunroof is a much more aerodynamic and efficient way to enjoy the view above.

How big is the trunk?

Many wedge-shaped cars have low hood lines and relatively large trunks. That's good, because the more things you can put into the trunk, the fewer things you'll need to put on the roof during highway trips. The EPA *Fuel Economy Guide* lists both interior and cargo space (in cubic feet) for new vehicles you may be considering.

Consider a wagon or crossover.

Consider either a conventional station wagon or a more trendy "crossover." The latter category defies definition but generally describes a vehicle that drives and handles like a car yet looks either like a tall station wagon or a relatively short (in height) SUV. Their cargo capacity is close to or exceeds that of many conventional SUVs, but their low roofline and small frontal area let them get much better fuel economy. In general, you won't be able to use them for off-road excursions, but you'll be able to haul lots of stuff without using the roof, and you'll be pleased when you visit the pump.

Fold-down rear seats.

Some cars have fold-down rear seats as either standard or optional equipment. With these, you can enjoy the fuel efficiency of a smaller car while being able to occasionally carry long or awkwardly shaped items that can extend into the trunk and which might not otherwise fit inside. If you're able to fold only half of the rear seat for a given job, this is even better, because you'll have the flexibility of being able to carry a passenger back there at the same time. This is one more way you can save gas by being able to put more things into the car instead of on the roof.

Climate and color.

To save fuel and still be comfortable, consider climate when you're selecting your car. If you drive in Arizona, for example, choose a light-colored interior and exterior. Your car will absorb less heat from the sun, so you'll make less use of the air conditioning. If you live in a cold climate, a darker color may be preferable, as you and your engine will need all the heat absorption you can get.

Take a showroom "trip."

If you're uncomfortable, you'll tend to be less patient and drive less efficiently while rushing to the safe haven of your destination. Given the pressure exerted on us by many vehicle sales consultants, what I'm about to suggest will be the equivalent of conducting your own assertiveness training course: Go to the showroom or lot, then simply sit in the car for at least 30 minutes. Consider the ambience, the comfort or lack thereof, the necessary positioning and movement of your arms and feet to operate controls, as well as interior quirks, protrusions, or seating characteristics that might not suit your size, shape, or preferences. Do not frighten the salesperson by bringing along a travel atlas.

Rent or borrow a twin.

If you don't really wish to sit in the showroom or lot for 30 minutes, and if you'd prefer something beyond the standard 5-minute test drive with an eager salesperson breathing down your neck, rent or borrow a car similar to the one you're considering for purchase. Then take it for a real test drive and get to know it.

Opt for a large fuel tank.

With a larger tank, you can take greater advantage of savings when you find a gas station with especially low prices. If you're looking at a number of different cars, and it's a close call, consider the fuel tank size and driving range. Finally, when you're on the road, it can be comforting to know you have enough fuel to get to where you're going.

Do you really need rustproofing?

Rustproofing compounds add weight, and added weight uses more fuel. Due to the increased use of aluminum and galvanized steel body panels in today's cars, rustproofing may no longer be as important as it once was. Yet, climate plays a role in this decision as well. If your local climate will expose your car to a lot of snow and road salt, then rustproofing might be a good idea.

Avoid auxiliary lighting.

Most new vehicles already come with excellent headlights, typically halogen or better, which are bright enough for most driving situations. Include a night-time test drive to be sure the low-beam pattern and intensity are to your satisfaction. Installing or opting for auxiliary lighting beneath the front bumper will add extra weight and consume electricity, both of which will increase your fuel consumption. Furthermore, unless you are one of the few people on the planet who actually has these lights aimed correctly, you are likely to induce anger and blindness among oncoming motorists.

Avoid power seats and windows.

Besides adding complexity and the possibility of future repair expenses, each of these items adds weight and uses electricity. Power windows may be part of an option package that includes a feature you really want, but it will probably be easier to avoid the power seats. According to Natural Resources Canada, the extra weight of power seats can increase fuel consumption by as much as 2 to 3 percent.

Splurge a little on the sound system.

With a good sound system and speakers, your trip will be more relaxing and pleasant. If you're in a good mood, this will enhance the unhurried mindset that safe and efficient driving requires. Caution: Avoid ear-splitting volume levels that will distract both you and neighboring motorists, and don't tap your accelerator foot to the music.

Remove bumper billboards.

If your state doesn't require a front license plate, you may find the dealer has installed his own plate where a front license plate would have been. Remove it as soon as you get home. This plate might assist your relationship with the dealer, but it will also tend to increase air resistance, and it could even interfere with proper engine air intake and cooling. Put it on the garage shelf and temporarily reinstall it whenever you need to return to the dealer for service, warranty repair, or a safety recall.

A curve at the plate.

If your state requires a front license plate on your new car, consider curving it slightly in at the bottom. This can improve your car's aerodynamics and fuel efficiency very slightly, but be sure to stay legal.

CHAPTER 5

Buying a Used Vehicle

Look for cars with efficient features.

When you're in the market for a used vehicle, you won't have the same ability to choose features as when buying new, but you can still look for cars with the kind of fuel-efficient equipment you'd like to have in a new vehicle.

What stage in the "model run?"

Buying a used car that was extensively revised from its preceding model year might be a bad idea. This was the model's rookie year, so to speak, and it could contain bugs that were fixed in later models. Unfortunately, many such bugs and problems seem to be associated with fuel, engine-management, and emission systems, all of which exert a strong influence on fuel efficiency.

Know where it's been.

Using the vehicle identification number (VIN), check CarFax or similar sources for a history of the car, including previous registration records with dates, places, and mileages. Many used car dealers will even supply the report for free. You may also learn about any suspicious events in the vehicle's past. Has it been in a major accident or submerged in a flood? A car that's been wrecked, abused, or remanufactured is not likely to be the fuel-efficient vehicle for which you've been looking.

Read *Consumer Reports'* annual auto issue.

Every year, *Consumer Reports* magazine publishes an auto issue that includes, among other useful information, listings of desirable and undesirable years and models of cars. Especially interesting are the reliability ratings charts that include seventeen potential trouble categories and how various years of a given model have fared on each. From an economy standpoint, the "Fuel System" segment would seem to be an especially important category.

Google the car.

These days, you can Google just about anything—why not the car you're thinking of buying? Type in the make and model, then add a few words or phrases like "problem," "how do I fix the," or "stall." The number and types of entries you obtain will give you some idea about the car's reliability, and the search will lead you to a variety of car sites, chat rooms, and news groups. You'll probably find some animated discussions and heated disagreements, but you may gain insight into a vital problem or issue that affects reliability or fuel efficiency. Remember to take online advice with a grain of salt—being on the Internet doesn't mean that something is true.

Use the NHTSA database.

Refer to *www.nhtsa.gov*, the U.S. National Highway Traffic Safety Administration's site for information on service bulletins and manufacturer recalls that could affect your prospective car's safety in general, and the fuel system in particular.

Other useful sites.

Two of the many other sites that can provide useful information on your potential used car are *www.edmunds.com* and *www.cars.com*. You may already be familiar with these sites and others. Favorable and unfavorable owner comments are typically abundant and sometimes presented in a brutal fashion. As always, be especially vigilant regarding information and problems related to the fuel system.

Does the car want to go straight?

If you're driving on a flat road, there is no crosswind, and you're traveling in a straight line, very briefly take your hands off the wheel and see if the car veers to either side. If it does, this could be a sign of tire pressures that differ from one side to the other, an alignment condition that needs adjusted, or suspension damage. The latter two possibilities are especially detrimental to current and future reliability and fuel efficiency.

Is the steering wheel off-center?

When you're driving in a straight line on a flat road, the steering wheel should be very close to the center position—in other words, if there are two opposing spokes, they should be nearly horizontal. If the steering wheel is far from the center position, it's possible that the alignment may be off or the suspension could be damaged.

Check the tire population and condition.

If the odometer shows very low miles, be suspicious if the car has three different brands of tires on it. The odometer may have been disconnected or "rolled back." Extensive wear on the outside edges of the front tires may reflect either hot-rod cornering or alignment neglect, either of which should be a red flag. If the previous owner didn't pay much attention to tires and alignment, there's a good chance he or she was not very vigilant about other aspects of maintenance as well, and you could end up with an inefficient engine that's only had its oil changed every 20,000 miles or so.

Is paint supposed to be there?

Body shops are very good at repairing cars that have been in minor and not-so-minor accidents. This makes it difficult for you to spot indications of previous repairs. One simple thing you can do is look for paint on things that were not originally painted at the factory— e.g., the underside of rubber weather stripping on the exterior of the car, especially the front. If a car has had extensive front-end repairs, run away as fast as you can and find an efficient vehicle that's still factory-pure.

"As-is" is pretty final.

Whether you're buying from a dealer or from a private owner, keep in mind that "as-is" means the car is still yours even if you have to refill the gas tank three times on your way home. If you're not ready to take the risk, buy a new or a certified used car of the same make and model. When it comes to a bad used car, fuel efficiency might be the least of the problems you encounter.

Reading the private seller.

If you're buying used from a private party, look for an honest-looking person with a cat on his lap, or someone with a stack of receipts supporting his contention that routine maintenance and service operations have been carried out with clockwork regularity. He or she may even refer you to the dealer service department so they can verify the soundness of the vehicle. On the other hand, if the owner has no receipts but claims to do his own maintenance, ask some questions about things like the location of the oil filter, the number of quarts the crankcase holds, or the gap to which the spark plugs are supposed to be set. Naturally, you want to ask how many miles per gallon the owner has tended to obtain in city and highway driving. If you sense some "dancing" in response to any of these questions, walk away.

Let your mechanic check it out.

The previous recommendations in this chapter are only the tip of the iceberg when it comes to examining the condition and quality of a used car. Probably the best thing to do is limit yourself to background research, then have a trusted mechanic examine the car from front to back and from top to bottom. You'll be charged a modest fee, but this will be very small compared to the increased confidence you'll enjoy when reaching your eventual decision about the car. The mechanic might even find some minor problems that are easily fixed but which could help lower the price. If you're thinking fuel efficiency, you may as well be thinking checkbook efficiency as well.

CHAPTER 6

Buying Aftermarket Accessories

Avoid "miracle" gadgets.

The Environmental Protection Agency has tested more than 100 supposed gas-saving devices and found very few that provide even marginal improvements in fuel efficiency. According to the EPA, some of the devices can actually damage the car's engine or cause the vehicle to fail emission tests. Stay away from products sporting claims that seem too good to be true. They probably *are* too good to be true.

Bug deflectors: do your homework.

In theory, the plastic shields that go on the front of your hood are intended to deflect air, bugs, and small stones over the windshield instead of into it. In practice, it all depends on which type of vehicle you drive and which types of deflectors are available. Some shields may only increase the effective frontal area of your vehicle, forcing it to make a bigger hole in the air through which it is traveling and reducing your fuel economy. On the other hand, driving efficiently requires good vision, and frequent stops to remove bugs from the windshield will also tend to reduce fuel economy. As always, it's your gas, your money, and your choice, so do the best research you can before making your decision.

Get a pickup truck bed cover.

Dogs love to ride in the back of pickup trucks, and part of the reason is all the air turbulence that's blowing around back there. Such turbulence exerts considerable air resistance and reduces fuel efficiency. With the bed cover, there may be a slight amount of flapping, but the air will pass more easily over the bed of the pickup instead of buffeting around within it. For better gas mileage, get the bed cover. If you want your black Lab to continue his enjoyable rides, either buy a motorcycle with a sidecar or find some other way to save fuel.

Ground clearance lift kits.

These are handy for off-road driving and clearing most of the rocks and other obstacles involved in such use, but the higher ground clearance will greatly increase under-vehicle air turbulence and greatly decrease fuel efficiency at highway speeds.

Towing packages.

Installing towing hardware on your vehicle will add weight, and the vehicle's aerodynamic and handling characteristics may suffer during the actual towing process. The weight of the trailer and its contents will also reduce fuel economy, of course. However, if you've purchased a towing package, it's undoubtedly because you sometimes need to tow something. If you do have a towing package on your vehicle, and you're not going to be towing anything very soon, save some weight by removing any components that are easily taken off and replaced. These may vary, depending on your installation, but at least remove the hitch ball component. Even a couple of pounds can help make your vehicle lighter and more fuel efficient.

Aerodynamic aids.

Aerodynamic aids such as front air dams and rear deck spoilers can help reduce air resistance and drag, thus leading to improvements in fuel economy. However, consider the nature of the device you are considering and the purpose it will serve. If the air dam or spoiler is solely for the purpose of exerting a downward force on the car to make it handle more securely at high speeds, the device could actually reduce fuel efficiency—this extra force will be transferred to the tires, which will in turn experience a heavier "load" and respond with greater rolling resistance.

Choose the right ski racks and bicycle carriers.

If you can, buy a bicycle carrier that can be temporarily installed on the rear of your car. When you're not hauling bikes, you can remove it, and when you are, they'll create less aerodynamic drag than roof-mounted racks or carriers. For ski equipment, some vehicles offer the ability to fold the rear seat or its center armrest so that skis can be placed in the trunk and extend partially into the passenger compartment. Naturally, this is much more fuel efficient than carrying them on the roof of the vehicle. In any case, don't mount ski racks or bike carriers except when you're actually using them to carry skis or bikes.

Buy a sunroof wind deflector.

If you've had an aftermarket flip-up sunroof installed in your car, and you did not purchase a wind deflector at the same time, you've probably noticed a lot of wind noise and turbulence inside your car. This can increase your car's air resistance. Get a Plexiglas glue-on or clip-on deflector and enjoy the open air more quietly and much more efficiently.

Avoid clip-on flags.

It's not unusual to see national flags or sports pennants clipped on to one or more of the side windows of a vehicle. The intention may be good, but the effect on fuel economy is bad. At highway speeds, flags and pennants flap crazily, and tend to exert the same amount of air resistance as extending one or two ping-pong paddles from the side windows. It's much more fuel efficient to display items or symbols within the car instead of having them flapping about on the outside. According to a study by a professor at England's Manchester University, the extra drag from two soccer-boosting flags can reduce fuel economy by as much as 3 percent.

Get rid of antenna decorations.

At highway speeds, cartoon characters, streamers, and other decorations mounted on the end of your antenna tend to have two results: a bent antenna and greater air resistance that leads to lower fuel economy.

Consider an engine block heater.

If you live in an extremely cold climate, you may actually need an electrical engine block heater just to get your engine to turn over and start. Because it helps warm your engine, you'll get more miles per gallon during those critical first few miles, a period when the fuel efficiency of any car tends to be horrendous. According to Natural Resources Canada, a block heater need only be plugged in or turned on a couple of hours before starting the car, and for a single short trip when outside temperatures are around 13 degrees Fahrenheit, you'll be using 25 percent less fuel.

Get extra window tinting—but keep it legal.

This could be a matter between you and law enforcement authorities in the jurisdictions where you live or through which you drive, as state and local regulations may vary on the amount of tinting that is permitted. However, windows that are even slightly tinted will help reduce the load on the air conditioner and provide better fuel economy.

Solar panel electrical helpers.

We will be seeing more of these devices in the future, since they can supply free electricity for a variety of functions, including keeping batteries charged and ventilating interior air to help avoid heat buildup. An electricity-generating solar sunroof is already available as an option on the third-generation Toyota Prius. In general, getting electricity from the sun means that we don't need to get as much of it from an alternator or generator that's powered by the gas we buy.

Buy a dashboard compass.

Long associated with older drivers, a trusty compass in the center of the dash is the precursor to today's modern navigational systems. If you don't have a GPS unit, and you're traveling in an unfamiliar area, it's nice to at least know whether you're headed in the right general direction. Fuel efficiency doesn't mean much when you're going the wrong way. If you're a youngster who would like to avoid the age connotation, get some Velcro patches and mount the compass only when it's needed.

Parents: consider a rear-seat DVD player.

To a driving parent or other adult, there are few things more irritating than hearing "Are we there yet?" Long after the kids have tired of playing "count the cows," their enjoyment of a movie in the back seat will make a journey more pleasant and help you be more patient and drive more fuel efficiently.

APPENDIX A

For the SUV Owner

If you own an SUV, you're getting the flexibility afforded by all that space inside, and it's comforting to plan a trip knowing you'll have little trouble taking along everything you need. On the other hand, as you're already painfully aware, gas prices are making it more difficult to afford that trip in the first place. In addition, you're probably having to field some questions from friends about your vehicle's thirst for fuel, and you may even be getting some unfriendly glares from others during your everyday trips and errands.

This is a book about fuel efficiency, not politics, so we will assume you actually need the space, the size, the ruggedness, and perhaps even the off-road capabilities your SUV provides. Nevertheless, the bad news is that you're using a tremendous quantity of gas and spending a lot of money on it. The good news is that the more you're spending, the more you could be saving. A 5 or 10 percent improvement in your fuel efficiency translates into a lot more money than for your neighbor who's driving the 35-mpg subcompact, and by following the advice in this book, you can get the most you can from what you've got.

Because your vehicle has a large frontal area and a boxy shape, high speeds will impose an especially great loss of efficiency due to the tremendous increase in aerodynamic drag as you travel faster. Granted, you may have a powerful engine that allows your SUV to easily overcome the inordinately high air resistance of high speeds, but this victory will come at the expense of an inordinately high rate of fuel consumption. Keep in mind that the horsepower required to overcome air resistance is a cube function of speed and, as explained in Chapter 1: Driving Efficiently, a 10 percent increase in speed will require a 33 percent increase in the horsepower you're using (and feeding) simply to overcome the resistance of the air through which you're traveling.

A lot of SUVs are very heavy, and yours is likely no exception. This makes it extremely important to conserve momentum by anticipating what's going on ahead, then reacting both early and appropriately. In many situations, the appropriate reaction to the clues ahead will be to lift from the accelerator as soon as possible. The sheer mass of a larger SUV makes brake avoidance and conservation of momentum especially important in getting the best gas mileage you can.

At steady speeds, greater weight will not be quite so harmful, but the fact remains that greater weight will require extra energy to start, stop, accelerate, or decelerate. To get the most from your SUV, pay special attention to anticipating the conditions ahead, avoid excessive speeds, try to keep your speed steady during highway travel, and think ahead so you can avoid or minimize use of the brakes.

APPENDIX B

For the Hybrid Owner

OK, so you've purchased a hybrid and helped save both your bank account and your planet. You're done now, right? Wrong! Many of the techniques throughout this book will help you do even better, even though your vehicle is already very fuel efficient. The electric motor/generator, batteries, and braking regeneration system work well together and perform seemingly miraculous feats, and the aerodynamic shape of the body plays a positive role as well. Perhaps the most exciting feature is the regenerative braking system that helps slow your vehicle by transforming the kinetic energy of movement into the electrical energy that's stored in that giant battery pack. This feature, along with the naturally low air resistance in urban driving, helps explain why yours and other hybrids might actually get better fuel mileage in stop-and-go city driving than they do on the open road.

Again, congratulations on recognizing and adopting one of the most significant automotive technologies to come along since the invention of the tubeless tire. Ever since the very first motor vehicle was produced well over 100 years ago, both valuable momentum and brake linings have been completely wasted by transforming movement into frictional heat and brake lining dust. Thus, this new technology and its incredible contribution to the conservation of fuel and energy is a pleasantly welcome feature for automotive engineers and drivers alike. In addition to saving fuel and money, receiving a degree of ecological satisfaction, and having a pleasant driving experience, you may further enjoy the technical pleasures of advanced dashboard instrumentation that allows you to precisely monitor your vehicle's fuel-saving modes and activities, as well as its energy consumption.

However, there are some other things to consider. For example, if you're driving nonstop across Iowa or Nebraska, your hybrid will tend to have very little advantage compared to other vehicles, because the rest of us don't use our brakes much anyway during this steady-speed driving. However, you *will* have a great advantage during steady cruising if the designers of your hybrid pursued the highly admirable goal of combining a very small and efficient conventional engine with a large supplemental electric motor. The small conventional engine and long-legged gearing will serve you quite well in steady-speed driving, even at interstate speeds. On the other hand, if your hybrid has a large conventional engine, it could be at a *disadvantage* during steady interstate cruising compared to non-hybrid vehicles of the same size equipped with a smaller and more efficient conventional engine.

In addition to anticipating conditions ahead and doing many of the other things we recommend in this book, you should be especially careful not to make excessive demands on the brakes. To a large extent, braking will transform kinetic energy into electrical energy for later use. However, when you make a panic stop or otherwise greatly stress the brakes, the regeneration system will not be able to handle this much need for stopping power, and less of the kinetic energy of movement will be transferred to the batteries. Be sure to brake gently if you need to brake at all, and keep in mind that the conversion from kinetic energy to electrical energy will not be 100 percent efficient. Although regenerative braking will be more energy-conserving than braking in a conventional vehicle, it will always be less efficient than not having applied the brakes at all.

APPENDIX C

The More Miles Per Car (MMPC) Factor

The techniques and ideas in this book not only help you save money at the pump, they also help you get more from your car and more *for* your car. After all, you will be selling it one of these days, won't you?

While you own it.

As you drive it over the miles, your car will appreciate that you've read and are applying the ideas in this book. Efficient driving is smooth driving, and smooth driving puts less wear and tear on the mechanical components. Engineers and mechanics will appreciate the unhappiness that jackrabbit starts and jerky driving inflict upon the engine, transmission, brakes, and others of the approximately 15,000 components that make up your car. Your smooth habits will help the gears to mesh together more comfortably during upshifts and downshifts, your brake pads and rotors will last longer, and the money you save on gas will be complemented by the money you'll be saving on parts, replacements, and repairs. In addition to the mechanical benefits, your enhanced awareness of and smooth responses to the traffic patterns around you will lower your probability of an accident, and should help keep both your insurance premiums and your body shop bills low.

When you sell it.

If you sell through the Internet or by classified ad, the prospective buyer will be able to see either your collection of maintenance receipts or (if you're a do-it-yourselfer) the maintenance log containing details about dates, mileages, and services performed. CarFax reports and checks by independent mechanics are always useful to a potential buyer, but talking to an honest owner who knows and cares about his car is definitely a comforting factor that opens the buyer's wallet.

If you sell to an individual, be sure to take him or her for a test drive in which (1) you drive first, and (2) you demonstrate your smoothness and skill in not abusing the car. The combination of your honesty, maintenance evidence, and driving technique will go a long way towards your getting the price you deserve for the car you treated so well. On the other hand, if you do a trade-in, you'll get closer to wholesale, but your care over the years will help ensure that the car at least starts and runs properly when the used-car manager appraises its value. If you've driven intelligently, efficiently, and unaggressively, as we've advised, your trade-in will further hold its value because the bumpers and body panels will have fewer dings, dents, and bashes compared to vehicles traded by those who are less enlightened.

"Hypermiling": Worth the Risks?

Back in the grand old days when British roadsters roamed the countryside and local sports car clubs were active and in abundance, enthusiasts often engaged in no-holds-barred contests called "economy runs." Participants pumped up their tires to rock-hard pressures to minimize rolling resistance, turned off their engines and coasted down hills, drove at low speeds that enraged the motorists behind them, and threw out everything but the horn button to minimize weight. Other unmentionable acts were performed, both in the garage and on the highway, all for the purpose of maximizing one's miles per gallon and winning a fancy pewter cup. Even with those low-tech cars of yesteryear, participants achieved levels of fuel efficiency that doubled or tripled what could be achieved today by the average person in his or her average car.

The scoring was simple. The tank was filled at the beginning, sealed, then refilled after the course had been completed. Naturally, cute little tricks sometimes entered the game. For example, a very serious contestant might get halfway through the course, then kick a dent in his gas tank so it would hold less fuel during the refill measurement at the end. Nothing was missed in participants' efforts to get the most out of their sports or economy cars, including such practices as placing masking tape over the gaps between the hood and front fenders in order to reduce air resistance.

The point of this trip through history is that we have a group of modern-day fuel economy enthusiasts who are also very good at getting the absolute most from a gallon of fuel. They are sometimes referred to as "hypermilers," and they are very proud of that label. They and their exploits are often described in online and print sources.

Hypermilers apply many of the driving techniques described in this book, but some of them routinely employ driving strategies that go far beyond what most safety experts would ever recommend that you apply during your own travels on public highways. For example, although you might get excellent fuel economy while meandering down a crowded interstate highway at 45 miles per hour, you would likely be able to do so for only a short time before you were either flattened by an eighteen-wheeler or made the unfortunate victim of a road-rage incident.

From an interest and purist standpoint, it's alright to understand and have some appreciation for the efforts of the old-time economy runners as well as the modern hypermilers. We all would like to get greater fuel economy and save at the pump. Fuel efficiency may be important, but the most important thing in driving is to do it safely, so a very important disclaimer is in order here:

For the welfare of yourself, your passengers, and your fellow motorists, please do not engage in driving or vehicular-modification activities that are unsafe, discourteous, or outside the law.

Sorry to be "preachy," but safety and lives are much more important than fuel efficiency and dollars. Stay safe out there.

Paper, Plastic, and the Price of Gas

Economics students learn early on that supply and demand have a lot to do with price. For a given supply of something (e.g., oil), increases in demand lead to increases in price. One of the ways you can save money at the pump is by doing things that decrease petroleum demand and encourage lower prices at the pump. Naturally, your contributions can range from minor to major. Here are just a few of many possible ideas for readers who are both environmentally conscious and interested in reducing the demand (and price) for that finite quantity of petroleum that will eventually run out.

A Google search uses oil?

We'll begin with a relatively trivial example. A Harvard physicist has determined that doing two Google searches has about the same carbon footprint as boiling a kettle of water for a cup of tea. The power for the servers responding to your Google search command comes from electricity, and about 1.2 percent of the electrical power in the United States is generated by petroleum. As we said, this one is kind of trivial, so don't lose much sleep or feel too guilty about your Googling habits.

Bottled water.

Besides costing more than the water it contains, the everyday plastic water bottle uses up a lot of petroleum in its manufacture. It has been estimated that bottled water containers account for about 2.7 million tons of plastic per year, that the plastic itself uses up about 17 million barrels of oil per year, and that this amount of petroleum would be able to power approximately 1 million automobiles during that same year. Although the plastic bottles are marked as recyclable, it has been estimated that only 25 percent of the bottles are actually recycled, with the remainder ending up in landfills or littering the environment. Based on the research leading to these estimates, it seems that less consumption of bottled water would lead to lower demand for petroleum products, which in turn would tend to lower the price for petroleum and its gasoline byproducts. How seemingly strange that a link, albeit slim, might exist between consumption of bottled water and the price we pay at the pump?

Paper or plastic?

Actually, a reusable cloth bag is the most environmentally kind bag to take with you to the grocery store. Both paper and plastic have their ecological downsides, and many consider paper worse than plastic. In the case of plastic, it has been estimated that Americans throw away nearly 400 billion plastic bags each year, with all these bags requiring millions of barrels of petroleum for their manufacture. Incredibly, it has been estimated that the average car could drive 1 mile on the petroleum used in the manufacture of just 14 plastic bags.

Geopolitics, Technology, and Pain at the Pump: And You Think We Have It Bad!

We don't get much sympathy from most other countries when we complain about what we have to pay at the pump. Drivers in European countries would simply *love* to be able to buy fuel at even the highest of the prices we've had to cough up. For the years 2008 back through 1995, these were the average annual prices (in U.S. dollars per U.S. gallon) for premium unleaded gasoline in the United States compared to prices being paid by some of our friends in Europe:

YEAR	ITALY	FRANCE	GERMANY	SPAIN	UNITED KINGDOM	UNITED STATES
2008	$7.63	$7.51	$7.75	$6.13	$7.42	$3.52
2007	6.73	6.60	6.88	5.36	7.13	3.03
2006	6.10	5.88	6.03	4.84	6.36	2.81
2005	5.74	5.46	5.66	4.49	5.97	2.49
2004	5.29	4.99	5.24	4.09	5.56	2.07
2003	4.53	4.35	4.59	3.49	4.70	1.78
2002	3.74	3.62	3.67	2.90	4.16	1.56
2001	3.57	3.51	3.40	2.73	4.13	1.66
2000	3.77	3.80	3.45	2.86	4.58	1.69
1999	3.87	3.85	3.42	2.82	4.29	1.36
1998	3.84	3.87	3.34	2.80	4.06	1.25
1997	4.07	4.00	3.53	3.01	3.83	1.42
1996	4.39	4.41	3.94	3.32	3.34	1.41
1995	4.00	4.26	3.96	3.24	3.21	1.34

Please note that the German price is for regular unleaded gasoline. Source: U.S. Energy Information Administration, Annual Energy Review 2008, p. 321.

Over the years, if we had to pay the kinds of prices they pay in Europe, we'd be driving the kinds of cars they tend to drive in Europe. About half of all vehicles sold in Europe are diesel powered, and the majority of cars have economical four-cylinder engines. Also, if you looked at this table and noticed a distinct upward jump beginning in approximately 2003, you're correct. The world is a complicated place where both planned and unplanned events can have a great impact on the gas-budget section of your wallet.

Expecting the unexpected.

During 2010, a lot of press was devoted to the Somali pirates who ventured far out to sea in their tiny fishing boats, then boldly hijacked huge cargo ships—a great many of them, in fact. They demanded and usually received millions of dollars in ransom for the ship, crew, and cargo they had seized. Naturally, giant oil tankers were not immune from the actions of these pirates, and we are fortunate that major environmental or minor economic catastrophes did not result from the taking of these kinds of commercial vessels. Piracy activities continue off the Somali coast, and their ranges have extended to more distant maritime regions. They and potential imitators could possibly end up attacking luxury cruise ships, private yachts, and commercial fisherman as well as the cargo ships and oil tankers that have been their usual prey. Although Somali piracy has occupied much of the news in the recent past, other geopolitical events could easily dwarf the economic and oil-supply effects attributed to these modern-day thieves of the sea.

As just one example, let's consider the Middle East, particularly the vulnerable Strait of Hormuz. The Strait of Hormuz, located between Oman and Iran, is just 21 miles wide and connects the Persian Gulf with the Gulf of Oman and the Arabian Sea. Each day about 17 million barrels of oil, representing 40 percent of all seaborne oil and 20 percent of all oil traded worldwide, are carried through this narrow passage in the midst of one of the most politically divided and diplomatically fragile regions of the world. About fifteen oil tankers per day travel through the strait, mostly to supply Asia, the United States, and Western Europe. Considering the vital importance of this single region of the sea, we have no choice but to reluctantly join oil market speculators in being concerned whenever any adverse events threaten the security of the strait. Of all industrialized nations, Japan has the most to fear, as 75 percent of that nation's oil supplies must pass through the Strait of Hormuz. If the strait were shut down for any reason and for any length of time, our own fuel prices would skyrocket, but the Japanese would find themselves in an especially dire predicament.

Regardless of how you feel about the existence of global warming, the fact remains that the oil-rich Gulf of Mexico and the unpredictable violence of our annual hurricane seasons can play havoc with both oil-trading speculation and the prices we end up paying at the pump. Oil companies are being forced to drill deeper and deeper in their search for remaining oil reserves in the Gulf, and it is said that the next great challenge is to bring up oil that may lies 10,000 feet or more beneath the surface. This is not an easy task—in a *New York Times* article, the following analogy sums it up quite well: "To picture the challenge, imagine flying above New York City at 30,000 feet and aiming a drill tip the size of a coffee can at the pitcher's mound in Yankee Stadium. Then imagine doing it in the dark, at $100 million a go." In total, the Gulf of Mexico accounts for 25 percent of U.S. oil production and 20 percent of our natural gas output.

If circumstances should combine all these deep-drill oil rigs and distribution pipelines with a few Category 5 hurricanes, you will most certainly have a gas-pump price explosion on your very own Main Street.

Ethanol and flex-fuel: a solution or a problem?

Combining renewable and corn-based ethanol with gasoline would, at first glance, seem to be a no-brainer in our quest for energy independence. According to Wesley Clark, a retired general and co-chair of the pro-ethanol group Growth Energy, "It's important for American national security to be less dependent on foreign fuels and to create jobs and to reduce greenhouse gas emissions . . . . For every billion gallons of ethanol we produce, that's a billion and a half dollars we don't have to spend on foreign oil."

On the other hand, while demand for renewable ethanol has increased the growing of corn in the United States, this has been accomplished by reducing the production of important global crops such as soybeans. Because the demand for soybeans has not declined, countries like Brazil have increased their own soy production to make up for the deficit. In the process, Brazil is said to have destroyed tropical rain forests to accomplish the greater soy production, and this has in turn destroyed the tropical forests' ability to absorb the carbon dioxide that many believe is thinning the earth's protective ozone layer and contributing to global warming. Hey, it's a complex and interrelated world out there—and it all has an influence on the price you pay after you hear the mechanized "ding-ding-ding" tones the next time you fill up at your local Gas 'n Go.

Speaking of gasoline and your local Gas 'n Go, the U.S. Environmental Protection Agency is anxious to raise the allowable 10 percent ethanol content to 15 percent, a seemingly inconsequential move that has drawn the ire and concern of engine and fuel system manufacturers. According to the Alliance of Automobile Manufacturers, increasing the blend rate above 10 percent (or "E10") would adversely affect vehicle emissions, performance, and durability. According to the automotive manufacturers, because the EPA has never required an ethanol content higher than 10 percent, they have never had a reason to design, test, or warrant vehicles for use with such fuels. I'm not sure about you, but I don't really care for my relatively new vehicle and its complex fuel and mechanical systems to be subjected to the uncertainties of field experimentation because politicians want to grow more corn.

Technology to the rescue!?

Observing America, most of the world would agree that we possess a unique ability—we rise to meet a challenge. Also, other nations, whether they like us or not, respect our ability to "think outside the box" in advancing and applying our considerable technological expertise to meeting such challenges. It's not just a coincidence that engineering and scientific students, as well as technical scholars, from all over the world gravitate to American institutions like Cal

Tech, Carnegie Mellon, Stanford, and M.I.T. for advanced knowledge in practically all forms of scientific theory and endeavors.

On a minor note, and speaking of the Massachusetts Institute of Technology, two M.I.T. graduate students have developed a simple but ingenious method for obtaining energy from the simple up-and-down gyrations of automotive shock absorbers. In addition to better cushioning of the jolts from wheels as they encounter potholes and other uneven highway surfaces, these shock absorbers generate electricity for use in powering the vehicle. These pioneering M.I.T. students claim their "regenerative" shock absorbers can increase fuel efficiency by as much as 10 percent, and they are already involved in field tests with the U.S. military. These shocks may well be standard equipment on one of the cars in your future.

On a more major and more immediate note, plug-in hybrids will most certainly be a part of your automotive future, and plugging in your car during the evening will become as commonplace as recharging your electric razor or your cell phone. Although hybrids are not yet a large percentage of the U.S. automotive population, they will grow in numbers and acceptance. To believe otherwise is the equivalent of betting that horse-drawn carts will make a comeback and replace the nearly 140 million automobiles currently plying our highways and byways. It has been estimated that, by 2020, hybrids will account for 25 percent of all automobile sales in the United States.

Of course, there will be problems to be solved. First, there are questions as to whether the nation's electrical grid will be able to handle the considerable load imposed by millions of plug-in hybrid owners all wanting to charge their automotive battery packs at the same time. Anybody over the age of fifteen is aware of brownouts, power grid breakdowns, and even international computer hackers who intentionally inflict damage and outages upon our system of electrical power distribution. However, advances in power grid management and the development of intelligent within-car charging systems offer much promise that these problems can be either minimized or overcome. The bottom line: even the worst-case scenario won't involve your needing a 20-mile extension cord to get to work a couple of decades from now.

Secondly, we'll need to consider from where the plug-in hybrids will be getting their electricity, plus the economic and environmental consequences of their receiving all this power. Currently, nearly half of our electricity comes from coal, a fossil fuel not exactly known for its environmental friendliness. Although we may aspire towards renewable sources of electricity, like wind, solar, and tidal power, the fact remains that the electricity we're using today comes from the sources shown below, and we will continue to rely primarily on these sources for a long time to come:

SOURCE OF U.S. ELECTRICAL POWER	PERCENTAGE OF U.S. ELECTRICAL
Power	
Coal	46.2%
Nuclear	21.0
Natural Gas	20.5
Hydroelectric	7.0
Renewable	4.1
Petroleum	1.2
	100.0%

Source: U.S. Department of Energy, via Andrea Stone, "Renewable Energy Plan Creates Rift," *USA Today*, September 8, 2009, p. 2A.

The current administration has vowed to create a clean-energy economy relying on renewable-energy sources like solar and wind power to largely replace traditional sources like petroleum and coal. For example, solar power installations might be placed in federally owned locations like the Mojave Desert, one of the sunniest places on the planet. In this context, we might add that the federal government owns some 20 percent of the land in the United States, mostly in the West. Environmental purists are opposed to littering pristine landscapes with wind-turbine farms and acres of solar panels, so there is no small amount of controversy here. The current administration's goal is to meet 25 percent of the nation's energy needs from renewable sources by 2025, compared to the Department of Energy's goal of 11.1 percent. Considering the parties involved and their disparate expectations, the potential for controversy and national debate is, to say the least, elevated. The bottom line: YOU!

As a society, if we continue to value neck-snapping acceleration and the ownership of conventionally powered vehicles that allow us to occasionally carry nine people and all their recreational toys, we are tempting fate, the environment, and our national security. On the other hand, if we adopt the old-fashioned American traditions of independence, invention, and problem-solving, we can get through what has been a very long period of oil addiction and move on to become a more efficient, a more satisfied, and a more secure nation. Please do your part by being more safe, more efficient, and less dependent on imported oil and the national insecurities that it entails. Be safe, be happy, and be green!

Sources

"100 Useful Web Sites," *PC World*, November 2008

T. C. Austin, R. B. Michael, and G.R. Service, *Passenger Car Fuel Economy Trends Through 1976*, SAE Paper No. 750957

Automotive News, July 18, 1966

Ashley Bates, "How Bottled Water Impacts the Environment," *www.gainsevilletimes.com*, September 9, 2009

Brad Bergholdt, "Monitoring Systems for Tires a Big Help," *Pittsburgh Tribune-Review*, June 6, 2009

Michael Cabantuan, "Driving 55 Can Save Gas," *The Indiana Gazette*, October 20, 2005

Thomas Content, "Alternative-Fuel Vehicles Save," *Pittsburgh Tribune-Review*, August 1, 2009

"Plastic Bags versus Reusable Bags," Dearborn County Soil and Water Conservation District, *www.dearbornswcd.org*, September 10, 2009

Tom Doggett, "Automakers Worry About More Ethanol in U.S. Gasoline," *www.reuters.com*, July 21, 2009

"Flag Drag Will Boost Fuel Costs," *www.news.bbc.co.uk*, June 21, 2006.

General Motors Corporation, *www.gm.com*

Giant Eagle advertisement for "foodperks" and "fuelperks," *Pittsburgh Tribune-Review*, June 7, 2009

Nanci Hellmich, "Obesity is a Key Link to Soaring Health Tab," *USA Today*, July 28, 2009

John Hult, "Texting-Driving Accidents Jump," *www.argus leader.com*, August 12, 2009

Maite Jullian, "Pedaling to Work Gets Push," *USA Today*, December 1, 2008

Clifford Krauss, "U.S. Asked to Increase Ethanol in Gasoline," *Indiana Gazette*, March 7, 2009

Michelin, *www.michelinman.com*

"A Bumpy Road to Efficiency," *MIT Technology Review*, May/June 2009

Jad Mouawad, "Drilling Deep in the Gulf of Mexico," *www.nytimes.com*, November 8, 2006

Natural Resources Canada, *www.nrcan.gc.ca*

"Carbon Emissions Up, Researchers Say," *Pittsburgh Tribune-Review*, February 15, 2009

"Perspectives in Carbon," *Pittsburgh Tribune-Review*, January 17, 2009

Matt Richtel, "U.S. Agency Withheld Data on Risks of Cell Use When Driving, Groups Say," *Indiana Gazette*, July 21, 2009

Press Release, Senator Charles E. Schumer (NY), August 6, 2003

Andrea Stone, "Renewable Energy Plan Creates Rift," *USA Today*, September 8, 2009

Tesla Motors, *www.teslamotors.com*

Tests conducted by the author for the Camping Trailer Division, Coleman Company, Inc.

www.theautochannel.com

Toyota Motor Corporation, *www.toyota.com*

U.S. Bureau of Transportation Statistics, *www.bts.gov*

U.S. Energy Information Administration, "World Oil Chokepoints," *www.eia.doe.gov*, September 10, 2009

U.S. Environmental Protection Agency: *www.fueleconomy.gov*, *www.epa.gov*, and *Fuel Economy Guide 2011*

U.S. Federal Trade Commission, *FTC Consumer Alert*, September 2005

U.S. Federal Trade Commission, *'Gas Saving' Products: Fact or Fuelishness*, July 12, 2007

Elizabeth Weise, "Ethanol Pumping Up Food Prices," *USA Today*, February 10, 2011

Bernie Woodall, "Plug-In Autos Charged Overnight OK for Grid," *www.reuters.com*, June 29, 2009

Chris Woodyard, "Tire Label Would Show Gas Savings," *USA Today*, June 19, 2009

Chris Woodyard, "Stick Shift's Not Getting Short Shrift," *USA Today*, November 5, 2008

Chris Woodyard, "100 mpg? Sounds About Right," *USA Today*, June 24, 2008

Index

watching other's brake lights in traffic, 1–2
Brazil, soybeans and ethanol issues, 177–78
Break-in effect, in new vehicle, 108
Bug deflectors, 151–52
"Bumper billboards," removing dealer's, 143
Cabin air filter, checking, 70
Campers, towing of, 101
Car Fax report, for used vehicle, 146
Carpeting, weight of vehicle and, 97, 133–34
Carpooling, 93
Cars, reducing number owned, 91
Cars.com, 147
Cell phones, 23
"Check engine" light, 67, 72
Chevy Colt, 114
Clark, Wesley, 177
Clothing, dressing for minimal use of air conditioning and heating, 22–23
Clutch
  free play in, 76
  keeping foot off when not using, 8
  replacing of, 77
CNG (compressed natural gas) vehicles, 116
Color choice, vehicle purchase and climate, 140
Compass, as accessory, 156–57. See also GPS navigation systems
Constant velocity (CV) joints, 82
Consumer Reports auto issue, 146
Continuously variable transmission (CVT), 121
Controls, learning to use, 24, 140
Convertibles
  managing buffeting and, 21
  sunroof as alternative to, 138
Cooling system (engine)
  checking hoses and cap, 77–78
  cleaning radiator, 78

electrically powered, 121
engine-driven cooling fan, 73
gauge on "C," 73–74
gauge on "H," 74
replacing coolant, 78
Cooling system (vehicle interior). See Air conditioning system
Corn, ethanol and increased demand for, 177–78
Credit cards, using oil company, 46
Crossover vehicles, 139
Cruise control
  disengaging of, 27
  new vehicle purchase and, 131
  using wisely, 26–27
Curves, negotiating efficiently, 15, 39
Cylinder deactivation, 120
Daytime running lights, 122
Diesel engines
  new vehicle purchase and, 115
  water separator in, 69–70
Diesel fuel
  foaming of, 51
  winterizing of, 47–48
Direct fuel injection, 120
Directions, asking for, 25
Disc brakes
  drag and, 34–35
  versus drum, 127
  maintenance and, 79–82
Dogs, open windows and, 21–22
Drag coefficient (Cd), 118
Drum brakes
  caring for cables, 35
  versus disc, 127
  maintenance and, 79, 82
DVD player, as accessory, 157
Edmunds.com, 147
Efficient driving, 1–44. See also Planning, for efficient driving
  acceleration, 2–3, 7, 13, 31–32